HOR

THE

COLLAR

By

A J Rowley

To Eira,

Happy reading.

Andrew.

Published in 2012 by FeedARead Publishing

Copyright © A J Rowley

British Library C.I.P.

A CIP catalogue record for this title is available from the British Library.

Dedication

This book is dedicated to my wife Angela, Alex, Faith and Andy, all of whom shared in different ways the joys, challenges, trials and tribulations of my ministry in Northern Ireland.

And with thanks to

Mark Burgess for reading the very rough first draft and for his comments, enthusiasm and encouragement throughout.

John Sanders, Jon Searle and Anna Martin for their proofreading of the text and helpful comments.

Ben Hollands, ex-student of mine and a very talented cartoonist, for allowing me to adapt his cartoon of me as *The Philosopher* for the front cover.

The Author

Andrew Rowley grew up in London's East End. He holds several degrees and post-graduate qualifications in Theology and Philosophy. He is a trained teacher, counsellor, NLP practitioner and liberal Christian minister. He is currently Head of Philosophy at an independent school. Andrew is married to Angela and they have three children.

Hot Under the Collar

By Andrew Rowley

Hot Under the Collar is an account of true events. At times it reads more like a script from *Father Ted*, *The Vicar of Dibley* or *Rev.* and some of the colourful characters involved might well have walked into the story straight off the sets of these much loved and hugely popular television series. But the events and stories recorded here are true and they have a darker context. *Hot Under the Collar* is set against the hostile and dangerous background of the Troubles in Northern Ireland.

It is a story about people and the rich vagaries of life. Some of it will make you laugh, some of it may make you cry and some of it will bemuse and bewilder you. There are tales of weddings, funerals, home visits and all the minutiae of church life; tales of bombs, bullets and "bandits;" tales of many eccentric characters, warts and all, and the attempts of a naive and overly enthusiastic young English minister to get to grips with a life most definitely foreign to him and his family. It offers a rich insight into a unique experience.

Andrew Rowley grew up in an agnostic East End family (his father had been born just around the corner from where the Kray twins lived and ruled). Andrew came to his liberal and open faith after a family tragedy, the death of his 17 year old brother in a car accident when Andrew was 16. After a fairly typical East End schooling and youth, misspent he says, Andrew left school at 16 with no qualifications to speak of (he was only allowed to take one O level, English, which he failed) and found work within the local authority as a clerical assistant and began his early career in finance and administration.

However, he never felt completely fulfilled in his working life. Following a 10 year quest exploring all manner of religious paths in an attempt to gain some spiritual insights, he felt called to serve people in a spiritual way. So it was he returned to education as a mature student to train for the liberal Christian ministry.

Six years, several qualifications and a teaching certificate later, now married to Angela, with two children, he completed his training. As part of it, from 1988 to 1990, Andrew, his wife and young family spent every college vacation in Northern Ireland, or the Province as it was often called, where he was employed as student pastor to Moneymore Church congregation on the edge of Belfast. When his training was complete he took up the permanent position there as minister.

Little did he know that on many occasions he would become very hot under the collar indeed.

Chapters

Page 10 Introduction

Page 14 My first dead body

Page 18 Almost caught naked in the manse kitchen

Page 23 "They (the IRA) will know you are here"

Page 27 An encounter with terrorists in the Mountains of Mourn

Page 32 Lost on the Falls Road and shooting in the Hospital

Page 38 More of death and what came next

Page 46 Fainting at the funeral and "calling at a rather difficult time"

Page 52 Home visits: much tea, many cakes, bowls of jelly and broken crockery

Page 63 Visits to the manse; a very cold manse, very slowly turning pink

Page 73 More home visits: two tangerines and a banana, the Zen art of knocking without knocking and the barn which wasn't there

Page 83 A lot of bull, huge hands and a giggle which would not stop

Page 90 Language problems and the "strange Wee-man"

Page 97 A very harsh accent, indeed

Page 107 A soldier crouching by a wall, a chilling advert and "First hang all the priests and then set them on fire, as just hanging is too good for them"

Page 115 A siege mentality and an eerie silence on the Shankill Road

Page 122 Weddings, a ride in a helicopter and "blown out of bed," or so she said, and still claims

Page 131 The wedding rehearsal and the bomb blast

Page 138 A long and bloody history and too close to home the atrocity at Loughinisland

Page 149 The massacre and what to do next?

Page 154 Meeting the survivors of a weeping and bleeding but unbroken community

Page 162 Back in the Manse, a day off which went wrong, a BBQ and nearly caught on the beer

Page 172 A near tragedy in the manse

Page 178 Free designer clothes and a gift: a wee drop of illegal drink

Page 187 The pub which opened just once a year

Page 196 The start of a desperate search for a curry

Page 202 A fake clerical collar and the search for a curry goes on

Page 211 Back in the manse: a meeting twice over, charity dispensed and vital money abruptly taken away

Page 217 The beginning of a particularly eventful evening in the manse: a tale of infidelity

Page 223 A suspected heart attack and a drink of Tipp-Ex correction fluid

Page 229 Special Services: a newborn lamb in church and "giving them the whole bloody bucketful"

Page 234 Seventeen "bad" eggs and offensive embryos, and "a bit too religious" for them

Page 242 A very noisy son welcomed accompanied by a very noisy band

Page 250 The service came to a messy end

Page 259 The day two donkeys and a pony came to church

269 A final tale: the worm turning in the light of the candles

Introduction

"How do you fancy going to Lebanon for the summer?" Andrew asked his wife one day on his return home from college. This was his way of softening her up. To her relief she found he was joking. To his relief she readily agreed his next proposal: a summer pastorate in Northern Ireland.

The plan was for them to spend eight-weeks there, with Andrew working at a church which had a membership of over 200 families, perhaps as many as 500 or 600 people; a congregation desperate to have a minister of their own again after several years without one; a congregation who were very keen when they heard there just might be a chance of a young minister-in-training, one with children as well, taking up the offer of a summer vacation pastorate with them. Not only had they been without a minister for several years, there had been no children in the manse for at least 70 years, with the last four or five ministers being elderly (and native to Northern Ireland).

Andrew was very keen. It was a chance to get some real hands on pastoral experience in a very difficult situation, but he was not quite sure how Angela would react to the idea, hence his opening question about Lebanon. For Northern Ireland was a place known to them simply through pictures in the media. Not quite Lebanon, but it was a place of bombs and bullets, and the lesser of two evils perhaps, for a young minister-to-be, his wife, two children and pet dog, Tessa?

Andrew and his wife Angela were born and grew up in the concrete jungle of London's tough and gritty East End – a far cry from the rural farming community on the edge of Belfast which made up most of what was to become his first church congregation. For two years Andrew and his family spent every vacation there, returning home to continue with his studies at Oxford. Towards the end of the first eight-week experience, somewhat overwhelmed by the warmth, generosity and genuine needs of the congregation, Andrew and Angela talked long and hard about returning on a permanent basis two years later when his studies were completed. The congregation were delighted that there was even the slimmest of chances of the family returning, of course; and they were extremely persuasive.

On the final evening of the first vacation pastorate, the congregation, wanting to leave a big last impression, arranged for the family to be in a nearby house under the pretext of a small gathering to mark their return to England. Then, at the appointed time, the family were led down the road to the church hall. There at the door to meet them stood a piper in full formal regalia, Scottish dress: hat, kilt, sporran, bagpipe and all; and much to their huge embarrassment the family were piped into a hall filled with over 300 of the congregation.

It was nothing like their East End upbringing. Speeches were given, egos stroked and presentations made to the family: gifts for the children, two, not one, but two, very large bouquets of flowers for Angela, and for Andrew a wallet stuffed with £500 in £5 and £10 notes, not an inconsiderable sum in 1988. My, did the congregation want them to return.

The evening entertainment, provided by church members, ended with a solo, an adaptation of the old traditional Scottish folk song dedicated to Bonnie Prince Charlie after his defeat at Culloden by the English, ironically, and his exile into France, expressing the hope that he would return to his people one day:

"Royal Charlie's now awa. Many a heart will break in twa, should he ne'er come back again. Better lo'ed you'll never be, will you no come back again?"

But the words had been adapted and now relayed a personal message and plea:

"Bonnie Andrew's going away, home across the sea." And the refrain, *"will ye no come back again."*

They sat there cringing, all eyes upon them, somewhat stunned as the 300 or more people joined in...

"Will ye no come back agin.....Many a heart will break in twa, should you ne'er come back again…….. Better lo'ed you'll never be, will you no come back again?"

Touched, but wanting the floor to open and swallow them up, they returned home bemused and wondering. They reached for a stiff drink.

But go back they did; several times. Returning three or four times a year during college vacations for the next two years until Andrew had finished his training, each time Andrew picking up where he had left off, visiting the congregation and the sick and hospitalised, helping out at funerals and weddings and conducting one or two services every Sunday. Andrew was paid student pastor rates. A great help at a time when they were very poor, living on a student grant, savings, housing benefit and preaching fees from taking up to three services each Sunday, which involved travelling from Oxford to churches throughout London, Essex, Sussex, Surrey and Kent.

On completion of his training the family relocated to Northern Ireland on the same day in July of 1990 that the Republic of Ireland football team were welcomed back into Dublin after their World Cup campaign under Jack Charlton. This made for a very interesting journey across Dublin where the narrow streets were thronged with cheering fans. Then it was up to the north, some 100 miles, across the border and into the Province of Ulster, using the ancient name for the region, or Northern Ireland as they knew it, and then home, or the place which was to be their home for the next few years.

My first dead body

"Do you want to see him?" she asked.

"Pardon," I replied.

"Do you want to see him?"

It took a few very long seconds before the confusing fog cleared from my mind and I began to make sense of what she was asking. A slight dread replaced my uncertainty. "Yes, of course," I replied.

We were standing in the hallway of a tiny terraced house in a small town just a few miles outside of Belfast. I had been in Northern Ireland for just a week, the first week of the first eight-week summer vacation placement as the student-pastor of Moneymore Church, when the telephone call came: a message from one of the most senior elders of the church, "There has been a death. You had better go to the house."

I climbed into my car and set off for the house, the death-house as it was now called. I wasn't really sure where I was heading as I had only very approximate and garbled directions. Neither was I sure what would be expected of me once I arrived.

A week earlier my wife Angela and I had packed up our old Citroen 2CV to capacity and beyond with our two children, dog Tessa and not quite all of our worldly belongings, for the eight-week stay. Every square inch of this rather small and certainly less than robust car (more like a motorbike with a tin canopy was how one of our friends had described this French creation) was filled to overflowing to the point that breathing in at the same time was a difficult if not dangerous experience for us all, including the dog. In addition, the horrendously expensive roof-rack covering the car's soft top (this bought especially for the occasion- only the special Citroen 2CV model would fit, so no cheap uni-part here!) was buckling under its burden. The 500cc engine, more suited to a medium size motorbike than a motorcar, struggled and strained to complete the 250 mile or so journey from Oxfordshire to the ferry port at Holyhead. Following a very, very rough three-hour crossing it was through customs and a very extensive search of the car and contents, and up from Dun Laoghaire to Dublin. Then, finally, the 100 or so mile stretch to the border at Newry, where the border crossing point was adorned with the rows of menacing, grey, armour plated police jeeps, complete with their rubber "skirts" designed to prevent petrol bombs sliding under the vehicle and exploding underneath, and on to Belfast, our destination.

Incidentally, the car did not survive the return journey. It got us there, it took us around the Province for the eight weeks, but it made the ultimate sacrifice as the journey home proved just too much for it, burning out the two pistons. In hindsight there was a poetic irony about this failure after a gallant effort. Perhaps it was a prophetic sign.

Now, less than one week after our arrival, ill-prepared after receiving virtually no training for the experience, and sorely lacking in insight as far as what to expect, I humbly stood there as the newly bereft widow asked me, "Would you like to see him?"

She was asking me if I would like to see her husband's corpse, which according to custom had been brought home for the final farewells a day or two before the funeral, a funeral which would invariably take place three or at most four days after the death. This was another huge difference to the practices in England where it was and still is not unusual for there to be a gap of up to two weeks or even longer between a death and the funeral.

"He's in there," she said.

"He's in there," she repeated, pointing to the door leading off the hallway into the front parlour, the room usually set aside for visitors and Sunday afternoon tea. She beckoned for me to follow her as she made her way to the door and slowly turned the knob. I followed on behind.

As we entered the dimly lit room my eyes adjusted. I could now make out the lines of the coffin. As we drew closer (it seemed to take an age), I could see the coffin was open. There was no lid on it. There inside, dressed in a smart, dark-grey suit, possibly the suit in which he had been married, was the neatly groomed and heavily made-up corpse, the first I had ever encountered. We stood in silence for a minute or two, heads bowed, amidst the flickering shadows thrown across the room by the one solitary candle.

Then the old lady turned to me and said something I will never forget. She turned to me and, in a proud and reverential tone, she pronounced, "Doesn't he look well."

****

I confess it was a surprise, a shock even, to encounter my first dead body in this way, especially as I had been given no idea at all that this might be the case. However, as shocks go it was moderate. I had been caught unaware, and not for the last time in Northern Ireland, and often it would be at times of death, but not always.

More than this, it was clear it was a question as well as a statement. One to which she expected me to reply. What could I possibly say to this? I did my best in what seemed a surreal few moments during which we discussed in some depth, and agreed, with me nodding solemnly and wisely, how well he looked. After a time of quiet reflection, the obligatory prayer and the gathering of some vital personal information to fit into my address at the funeral, I returned home and immediately had a large whiskey.

Almost caught naked in the manse kitchen

Another early experience, one which might have been truly shocking both for me and the dear lady concerned involved me in the manse kitchen wearing nothing but a very small hand towel.

"Yahoo. It's only me," came the high pitched and unmistakable tones of a voice well known to me: a friendly voice, welcome on the whole, under normal circumstances, but on this particular occasion a voice which made my blood run cold. It was Dorothy, the long serving Church Flower Secretary, and there I was standing naked with a pool of water forming at my feet on the cold, hard tiles of the manse kitchen floor.

Dorothy was a loyal and generous member of my church and another church as well. She also found the time to attend and support a number of other smaller satellite congregations, which was not unusual in this part of the world. Dorothy, it must be said, was a "well-churched" lady, totally committed to her religious faith, and she was as genuine and honest as they come. This could not be said about all of the rich and varied characters we encountered during our time in Northern Ireland. It was Dorothy who raised money at work to support my journey to Romania in an attempt to bring home either a baby or young orphan child following the harrowing scenes we had witnessed on our television screens of the torment and desperate conditions in many of the orphanages of Ceausescu's rule; it was Dorothy who came to support me in the early hours of the morning when I spent twenty-four hours in my church on a fast and prayer vigil to raise money for the starving people of Sudan; it was Dorothy who bought for the church Christmas festivities a large illuminated, plastic snowman, whose arm moved up and down in a friendly wave (no one had the heart to tell her that he looked terribly out of place in the centre of the church); it was Dorothy who had unfailingly for decades, through the changing seasons, as regular as clockwork, bought and arranged the flowers for the floral displays which stood adorning the pulpit of this 200 year old meeting house, all to the glory of God. It had been known for Dorothy to arrive at the church as late as midnight and beyond to do this if other business delayed her, for she would allow nothing to prevent her from carrying out her solemn duties. Now it was Dorothy who was about to see me naked.

Angela was out shopping with our children, I had been out visiting all day and had rushed home to grab some food, take a bath and change before setting off again to yet another committee meeting of some sort or another. I had just climbed into the bath when I heard the telephone ringing urgently. The telephone of the manse always rang urgently, or so it seemed, for it always brought some news, mostly bad or sad, which inevitably meant more demands on me to which I would respond with great diligence and enthusiasm as a young and newly ordained minister. I would drop everything and go and visit "my people," be it at home or in one of the several hospitals, such as the Dundonald, or the Royal Victoria on the Falls Road, the hospital where our son would be born to the sound of machine gun fire in August of 1991. This was the hospital of which it was said brain surgery expertise was second to none in the world because of all the practice the surgeons had gained over twenty-five years of the recent Troubles, sadly through dealing with the many victims of shootings and bombings.

And now the incessant ringing of the telephone broke into my ablutions. For a moment or two I tried to ignore it. It stopped. "That's okay," I said to myself. Then it started again with an increasing urgency and, so it seemed to me, a desperate plea to be answered. I remember doing a quick mental stock-take of all those of my congregation who were ill or worse, and I decided I must obey the call. Somewhat reluctantly, I climbed out of the bath and grabbed the nearest towel, a small hand towel, and I began the descent to the kitchen where the manse's solitary telephone sat. When I say descent I am not exaggerating. The manse was huge. At least it seemed so to me as I had been brought up in a two-up-two-down terraced house in London's East End. The manse was a double-fronted barracks of a place, with five large bedrooms and a grand hall and sweeping staircase, down which I ran, dripping and covered with the tiny towel alone to cover my blushes. I can still feel the chilly draft which greeted my hasty descent to reach the telephone before the messenger of doom gave up. Mind you, it was always cold in the manse.

The chilly draft was the last thing on my mind as I rushed into the kitchen and grabbed the telephone, oblivious to the second icy assault as I opened the kitchen door. I stood there and received the news: it was Mr Jones, one of my congregation, a farmer, an important member of the community and of the Orange Lodge; his wife had been rushed to hospital. Taking down the details, offering what words of comfort I could, I was mentally assessing the time it would take to make the visit into Belfast and how it would fit in with the demands of the meeting still to come that evening. And then I heard it. "Yahooooo. It's only me." Then, "Is anyone at home?"

My God, Angela must have left the front door unlocked, and here was Dorothy marching her way down the hall, attracted by the muffled sound of my responses to and comforting of Mr Jones, heading straight for the half-open kitchen door, behind which, across the distance of some four metres of cold, hard, kitchen floor tiles, stood her young minister, shivering in a pool of water, naked except for the small towel.

What happened next was like a scene from a comedy farce. I dropped the telephone which smashed on the tiles, cutting off Mr Jones in mid-conversation. I leapt across the kitchen, dropping the towel in my urgency and the speed with which I covered the distance. I arrived at the door stark naked just as Dorothy was about to step through it, and somehow I managed to throw myself against it, slamming it shut in her face, fortunately without causing her any damage.

It was a strange and muffled conversation which ensued as I tried to explain that I was alone in the house and that I had been in the bath and that I was on the telephone speaking to Mr Jones, whose wife by the way "had been rushed into hospital" and "was doing quite well, thank you," and I "could not open the door or come out of the kitchen because I was almost naked." I was sure she understood. Dorothy was a very understanding person. But she did give me a very funny look as I greeted her in church after the next Sunday morning service.

Such was life in the manse.

"They (the IRA) will know you are here"

"They will know you are here," said Rev Charles Kilty, turning his gaze up from the flickering flames of the coal fire to stare at us intently. "Oh yes, they will know you are here." These were the sincere, honest and chilling words of a very senior elderly minister who had come to welcome us very late on the night we arrived for our pastorate. He was referring to the Irish Republican Army, the IRA. This, at the end of a very long day; and, my, had it been long?

The day had started around 5.00am in our Oxfordshire village. We had been up very late the night before packing up the car with everything we could squeeze into it for the eight-week long trip. We woke the children, had breakfast, walked the dog and then set off for Wales and the ferry port of Holyhead. We allowed plenty of time for traffic jams, adventures or misadventures, but it was a quiet, easy and uneventful journey. It did take a long time, though, mainly due to the lack of power produced by the 2CV's tiny engine and the weight it was now expected to pull. Having travelled for over 18 hours, including six hours or more on the road to Holyhead, plus frequent stops to relieve, in one way or another, or feed children or dog, plus more than three and a half hours on the ferry itself, extensive custom checks on both sides of the Irish Sea, then a final three-hour drive north to Moneymore, we arrived at the manse in the dark. We finally settled the children and the dog in their new environment, after much excitement and some exploration of the place. It was well past our normal bedtime by this point and we were exhausted. We sat by the coal fire feeling light years from home.

We had just begun to chat over the day and what would come next, and there was a tap, tap, tap on the front window. Opening the curtains we saw the ghostly shape of Rev Charles Kilty, illuminated by the moonlight, dressed in the traditional charcoal-grey suit, black shirt and thin white strip of the clerical collar identifying him as a man of the cloth. A slim and wiry Ulsterman, who always had a story to tell about anything and everything, from the breaking-in of horses, his days with the travellers and the circus, the Troubles of course, and so much more; he seemed to us to be the archetypal Irishman. He was then well into his seventies and he seemed to spend all of his waking life visiting his congregation, that was when he was not doing some business with local farmers, or the travelling community, buying or selling some ducks or horses, an odd calf here and there, or a pig or goat.

"I have come to welcome you to Ulster," he announced, rather formally, ceremoniously extending his hand, and we were touched by his kindness and concern. We were also more than impressed by his stamina. He stayed for more than two hours, until well past 1.00am. Talking to us, at times at us, entertaining us with all manner of stories, telling us about the set-up of the church in general and this congregation in particular, warning us of the personalities in the congregation and amongst my clerical colleagues. At times he spoke of the wider political situation in the

Province, the latest shootings and the most dramatic and terrible atrocities of the past. He also told us some jokes. My, how he held court to the two strangers, who, by this time, could barely keep their eyes open, especially in the face of the heat of the fire. He told us the one about the parrot and the pieces of eight, referring to what sounded to us a terrible incident way back in May, 1972, when the premature explosion in the Short Strand area of Belfast killed four IRA members and four civilians; in other words eight from the other side of the sectarian divide, hence the "pieces of eight."

Our heads were reeling, rather. After all, we were over 500 miles from home, absolutely shattered and not sure at times whether we were expected to laugh at this and other jokes we thought more than a bit inappropriate. Then he bent forward and gazed into the fire and told us in all sincerity of the expertise of the intelligence and information gathering network of the IRA. "Second to none," he said, "even the British Army's." He continued, "They know everything you know: who is living here and who is living there; who is going there and who is coming here." We were not too sure where 'here' and 'there' actually were, but we got the point.

There was a lot of fire-gazing going on during this time, as if staring into the flames like it was some ancient oracle offered pictures of the distant past, opened up a revelation of the truths of the universe or insights into the future. Fire-gazing like this was a common experience of my visiting around the Province. Hours were spent sitting next to or in front of the ever present fire (essential given the chilly and damp weather which dominated) which seemed to captivate all.

Looking up from the fire, Rev Kilty gazed at us intently and said, "They will know you are here, you know." As if for effect he repeated it. "Oh yes, they will know you are here."

And he meant it. The room fell silent.

****

He left soon after, in the early hours, out into the cold and dark night. A strong, cutting and chilling wind blew through the manse. We closed the door, tight, and bolted it. Looking at one another we made our way up the large sweeping stairs, across the large and open landing, which could have taken another large double bedroom if one was needed, we checked on the children, twice, and went to bed.

In a strange bed, in a strange house, in a strange land, in the dark hours of the night, his words stayed with us. "They will know you are here." We did not sleep much that night, I can tell you.

An encounter with terrorists in the Mountains of Mourne

This was not the first time during the first summer pastorate that a story chilled us. An elderly couple, Bill and his wife Margaret, took us out for an afternoon drive into the Mourne Mountains, which truly did sweep down into the sea at Newcastle. Bill was a slow driver, creeping along the dual carriage way at 30 miles an hour in his old beige Lada, with his face pressed up close to the windscreen. He went even slower on single roads, causing a huge tailback of cars behind him. He was oblivious to it all. Then it was deep into the mountains. Margaret was a sweet lady who revealed more by her facial gestures and body language than anything she ever actually said. On more than one occasion when Bill, a truly honest and gentle soul, began to hint that the congregation were not, how shall I put it, as straight forward as we might first have thought, Margaret, squirming and frowning, would cut in, "Now then Bill, I think you have said a wee bit too much there." And with that Bill would clam up, obedient to the last.

Bill had been the Church Secretary for decades until a few years before and he had many rich insights into the complexities of the congregation and the personalities involved. He had seen how previous ministers had fared. He was one of those who believed me when, towards the end of my ministry in Moneymore, I informed the congregation that I had received a disturbing anonymous letter, obviously by its contents sent by someone in the congregation. Some doubted me, but Bill did not, because Bill had received one himself, some thirty years before. He knew what some of the congregation could be like. He told me that he had done with his letter what I had done with mine: he had thrown it straight onto the fire. Whenever he tried to tell us more, to warn us perhaps, Margaret would cut in and that was that. "Look there Mrs Rowley," she would say, changing the subject and pointing to an area with a sign boldly stating Picnic Area, "there is a picnic area."

Bill was allowed to tell us how on one similar journey one afternoon the previous summer, when he and Margaret were taking visitors from England on the exact same route deep into the mountains, they had come upon a small queue of cars. Thinking at first it was a broken down car ahead they sat and chatted; then Bill could make out the hooded men ahead working their way down the line of cars ahead of them, stopping at each, looking inside and talking to the occupants. This was no police or Army roadblock, something we all got used to, being stopped on a regular basis whilst going about daily life. This was the IRA or a splinter group. This was serious. The mountain roads and passes it was said were often used by escaping paramilitaries as a convenient and hard-to-police route from Northern Ireland over the border into the safety of the Republic. The smugglers of old had done it and now we were told the modern day "bandits," as they were called, followed the same practice.

Bill and Margaret said they did not know what to do. They realized they were in a very difficult situation. They were not just two elderly people out on an excursion, two elderly people who had strayed into a terrorist event. They were Protestants, and this was enough at certain times and in certain places to warrant an attack, even their deaths. It was not always one's political leanings, or views on a united Ireland or loyalty to the Union, which resulted in danger or worse. At times it was simply being in the wrong place, or the wrong part of town, at the wrong time. By birthright you were deemed to be from one side of the divide or the other and a legitimate target. Even having red hair could be seen as a sign that you were from the Irish-Catholic side, and, when tensions were high following some large scale atrocity, could be enough to trigger a negative reaction, at times with dreadful and terrifying consequences. There were enough examples of this from recent history.

We had a friend who was spat at in a Belfast shop and called a "Catholic bitch" simply because she had red hair. Even having the wrong name might do it. The name 'Seamus' told everyone you were probably a Roman Catholic, for example, and 'William' told them that you were probably a Protestant, or that you, "kick with your left (or right foot), as they often put it." Often, when the chips were down, people were seen to be from one side or the other, with no room for a moderate or neutral position, irrespective of real political persuasion or involvement. Any reasonable person would know that being a Roman Catholic did not automatically make one a Republican wanting a united Ireland and "Brits Out," as proclaimed in spray-

29

painted messages on many street walls. But to many this was the case. The divide was real and seemingly inescapable.

Poor Bill and Margaret did not know what to do. To make matters worse they had with them two passengers, visitors from England, and this at the height of the Troubles. They did not know what to expect and spent a few very uncomfortable moments while the hooded men worked their way down the line of half-a-dozen cars towards them. The visitors were struck dumb in the back seat. There was not much they could do, but wait.

The two hooded men approached the driver's window, and one of them tapped on it with the barrel of a handgun and motioned with it that Bill should wind down the window. He did not protest.

During the next few minutes it became clear that this was a highly organized search. The terrorists were obviously searching for a certain target. Fortunately, this was not a random tit-for-tat reprisal act for some recent atrocity carried out against their own community, the response which could be totally indiscriminate and victimize the most innocent of people, with age or gender affording no protection to the unfortunate subject. This was different. It was clear the men knew who they were looking for and that they were not interested in Bill or Margaret or their English guests, at least this time. Bill and Margaret were warned to be on their way and to make absolutely no attempt to contact the police or the Army. The tone of the warning made it quite clear that these men meant business, and Bob and Margaret thought woe betide the quarry, should they catch him, or them, whether it be it an off duty soldier or policeman, or woman, an informant or loyalist terrorist.

Fortunately, Bill and Margaret were unscathed by their experience and were quite happy to take us on the same route a year later and point out the exact spot this event occurred. It left us a little uneasy. I knew of members of my congregation who would dare not venture into this area, not even to visit the seaside town of Newcastle, the destination of many family visits for us and for many thousands of families each year. But for many this area, and areas like it, were too unpredictable, too close to "bandit country," as it was called.

I was also warned on a regular basis that I could be a target, especially when driving my old Skoda with its English number plates. This by then had replaced the 2CV. The 2CV had died on us after limping home at the end of the first summer pastorate. All we could afford to replace it was this old beige Skoda, which we brought across with us from England at the end of my training. It was often said by my concerned congregation that I could easily be mistaken for an off duty soldier and be seen as a soft target because of these car number plates, and because I was then quite young and slim, with a very short haircut. Each time the same words were repeated we recalled the horrific and terrifying TV pictures of the two soldiers being dragged from their car in Belfast and brutally murdered under the gaze of the world's media, not so long before.

Lost on the Falls Road and shooting in the hospital

"Off duty soldier;" these words were ringing in my ears as I left home one evening during the first week of my first pastorate to visit Mr Kerr in the Royal Victoria Hospital just off the Falls Road. I had been given approximate directions how to get there and warned about a certain stretch of road which I would pass near to, the Short Strand, a notorious ghetto of poor housing, said to be a Republican enclave. "Do not go in there," was the stern warning from more than one member of the congregation, "If you do, you will not come out alive."

Uncertain as to exactly where to go that night, I set off. Soon I was lost up on the Falls Road. I parked up, and I was a little dubious about what to do next. I wasn't even wearing the clerical collar which might have explained my presence in the area and offered me some protection. However, I was sure that I would not turn back and go home. After all this was God's work and I was full of faith and enthusiasm. So I wandered around trying to find my way to the hospital. I stopped and asked several people, and whilst I met with some strange looks, it was obvious I was not from around these parts, and on account of my strange English accent I had to repeat my request for directions more than once, I was finally pointed in the direction of the hospital and I found my way there.

All of this sent shock waves through my congregation when I reported back on my exploits the next day. I think they thought that I was not safe enough to be let out on my own in future, but I reckoned that even the most die-hard IRA terrorist would not think that an off duty British soldier would have been walking alone, lost and vulnerable in one of the most notorious IRA-run enclaves in the Province: a place where even the Army and police went only in convoys, mob-handed, armed to the teeth and battle ready, often coming under fire or the threat of petrol bombs.

As you can imagine I was relieved to make it safely to the hospital, but even then my education into the ways of the Province continued. The difference to England was made very, very clear, driving home to me how sinister Northern Ireland could be and the risks attached to the most innocent of events.

****

It was quite late when I arrived at the ward to see Mr Kerr that night. He was delighted to see me. It meant so much to him. He knew that I was new to the Province and English, and that I was venturing into a part of the city where many of his native countrymen would not go, or at least would feel very uncomfortable doing so and would have a great sense of relief to be leaving without incident. He was also racked with pain, moaning dreadfully, having had a suspected heart attack. There were at least two doctors around him, and two nurses. They stood around the bed and were treating him and prepping him to go down to theatre. He was in terrible pain according to his moans, but still he managed to try to sit up and extend an arm towards me and exclaim in a surprisingly loud and clear voice, "You came, your Reverence, you came." Then, all the while apologizing profusely that he could not stay and say more to me, he was wheeled out. He was still apologizing as he was wheeled down the corridor towards the lift which would take him to the operating theatre.

****

The office of minister was held in very high esteem indeed, for some a very real and tangible sign of things unseen, a representative of God. This high regard for ministry was completely foreign to me. My idea of ministry was not one of an elevated role, but more one of standing alongside people in some way to support them and share their burdens, especially when life brought them to their knees. The high view of ministry, putting the minister up on a pedestal, was strange to me, and I was not at all comfortable with it, being very aware of my own human foibles and failings.

****

When I returned to visit Mr Kerr two days later he was in bed recovering from his operation. He immediately went into a very long and again profuse apology of how sorry he was he could not spend time talking with me when I had taken the trouble to come all the way into the city to see him, with me being "strange to these parts," and "risking the Falls Road and all," all on his behalf. Indeed, I do not believe that I ever saw him again without him making reference to that first visit and how much it had meant to him. He always, without fail, proudly told this story to anyone who would listen.

The second visit was also an eye-opener and my education continued. Willie told me how lucky it was that I went in on the night I did because the previous evening there had been terrorist activity in the hospital itself. "You see," he explained to me, "the hospital sits just off the Falls Road but could be used as a cut through or escape route to the Shankill." The Shankill Road was the Protestant equivalent of the Falls, a poor area and a breeding ground for loyalist paramilitaries who, we were told by many, believed they were defending their Province and their people from the threat of the IRA and a united Ireland. The common view amongst many, including some of my own

35

congregants, was that without the Army, the security forces and the illegal paramilitary organizations the Protestant population of Northern Ireland would soon be, "swept into the sea."

****

The day after his surgery Mr Kerr was recovering in a four-bedded ward. Late in the day gunshots were heard from the floor below. Willie had already made friends with the occupants of the other beds and the issue of religion or politics had not been broached. Hospitalisation and pain are great levellers. Yet, each knew the standing and background of the other. Willie told me of the instant pact they made as they heard the shots. Jimmy, a Roman Catholic in the far bed immediately said, "If it is one of mine," meaning the IRA, "you say nothing, pretend to be asleep, and I will tell them that you are one of us." He continued with the other side of the bargain, "But if it is one of yours, I won't say a bloody word, and you had bloody better do the bloody same for me." It was good to hear that people from the opposing communities were able to work together in such a way. Fear and the will to survive can be a wonderfully unifying force.

As it happened the pact was not needed that evening as the terrorists being chased by the police or Army, or both, were using the hospital as a short cut through to their own safe area having created some mayhem in the opposing community. Apparently, I was told, the doctors and nurses at the Royal were used to such events and were quite proficient at lying down in the wards and the corridors to dodge any stray bullets which might come their way.

"Thank God Almighty you did not come to see me last night, your Reverence," said Willie, over and over again, as I was leaving to go home to the manse. After all of this, I, too, was glad to be leaving and soon driving safely away from the Royal, quickly past the Short Strand, and out of Belfast, towards home.

Little did I know –perhaps I should have guessed– that I was to come much closer to the darker, sinister side of Northern Ireland's Troubles than the events of that night.

More of death and what came next

After my encounter with the open-top coffin and the corpse I was always well prepared for a visit to a death house and very soon got to grips with what was expected of the minister visiting at such times. If the death was part of a long illness or old age, say, then I would have been in very regular contact with the person and the family, visiting every two or three days, even more often in the final stages.

At times, depending on the time and place (it might be in a person's home, in a hospital or a residential or nursing home) it would be me alone with the person preparing to take the ultimate journey into the unknown. These were special times, often taking place during the dead of night. I would never divulge the content of the more often than not heartfelt conversations which were shared. There were times when I would sit alone in the small hours at the bedside, listening to the laboured breathing, even the last gasps, of the imminent traveller. Hospital and nursing home staff were always so very supportive and discrete in recognizing the importance of this spiritual support to the person and his or her family, allowing us much undisturbed quality time around the necessities of the medical processes involved: the monitoring, the checks, the placing or replacing of tubes and wires, all carried out discretely as if I were not there.

When the inevitable came, I would be there for the family supporting them in their shock and grief the best I could. This continued over the days which followed: talking and listening, sharing the families and friends' memories of their loved one and listening to much 'craic' (pronounced crack), as it was called, an Ulsterism referring to a fun time and good conversation. It was rarely very sombre and sad throughout. Often light and funny stories from the past illuminating the deceased's character, even foibles, were shared in memory and tribute and to lighten the atmosphere. Often it would mean sharing long periods of silence.

****

When a death was sudden and unexpected I was expected to arrive at the house as soon as the news came through, pretty much at any time of the day or night, after dropping everything. I would be warmly welcomed by the family and join the throng of neighbours who had rallied to support the family at their time of need. I would spend a great deal of time sharing and supporting them all, and there was always a constant supply of tea and food to sustain us. At times of crisis, when there was nothing else that could be done, out came the teapot, hands put to work and minds occupied. A cup or mug of hot, sweet tea was a real, tangible and comforting symbol of support and more.

It was something to hold on to, and something to stare at during times of silent reflection.

The days before the funeral passed this way, with a stream of visitors calling in to deliver their tributes, pay their respects and offer their support, with a stream of tea, and food, flooding out of the kitchen to supply their needs. In essence it was the traditional wake.

Each visit, I would spend an hour or two at the home, mentally collecting up facts and anecdotes to help with my funeral address. This was especially vital in the early days of my ministry, or if the deceased and his or her family were not known to me. Then a repeat visit next day, and much communication with the undertaker with whom I would work closely to ensure that everything was carried out with dignity and according to the deceased and the family's wishes. These visits would continue in this manner until the funeral, usually taking place within three days, a huge contrast with the situation in England where it could be ten days to two weeks or more between death and funeral.

On the day of the funeral there would usually be three parts to the proceedings. I would arrive at the house in time to meet the coffin as it was brought home from the funeral parlour, unless it had remained in the home for the three or fours days and the wake. I would lead the coffin into the house with prayers. The coffin lid might be removed to allow a final farewell for those who wished for it. Then after a short service of prayers and readings the coffin lid was put on for the final time, the screws were inserted and firmly tightened down. Then, after leading the coffin to the hearse and watching as it was placed with great dignity inside, usually complete with dozens of wreaths and all manner of floral tributes, I sped off in my car to the church in order to make sure I arrived there first and in time to be gowned, composed and in place to meet the cortege. Whereas the service at the home was restricted to the family and close neighbours and friends, the service at the church was a much larger and open affair, complete with eulogy, readings, hymns and organist playing and so on. Again I led the coffin both in and out of the church, with more prayers, and then it was on to the graveyard for a good, traditional, Christian burial. Cremations then were comparatively rare, if not unknown, especially amongst the country folk, for whom tradition was the foundation, norm and security of life.

I was never less than amazed by the attendance at funerals in Northern Ireland. After my experience in England where I had often seen just one or two cars following the main cortege, or attended a cremation where there was merely a handful of mourners (the exception of course was always where the death was that of a young person) the stark contrast was very clear. It was not exceptional in Northern Ireland to have 300, 400 or 500, or more, mourners in attendance, oddly mostly men, all dressed very formally, in black or dark grey suits, more often than not almost all wielding, almost weapon-like, a black umbrella. It rained a lot in Northern Ireland. At times it seemed that the whole village or area had turned out to pay their respects. As it did not seem to me possible, especially with my background being the East End of London, that everyone could have known the deceased so very well, I did wonder at times if there was some sort of unwritten pact in these parts, "I will go to your funeral if you go to mine," thus ensuring a jolly good send-off for all. For there did seem to be some satisfaction and pride for all concerned in a having a church full to overflowing on these occasions. More likely, it was a sign of close-knit communities, which paid their respect to the deceased and offered support to the family at their time of need.

For me, in the early days, as an inexperienced and then only partly trained minister, it was a huge pressure to take part in these events. At best, emotions were always high, as the story below about the traveller family will demonstrate. At worst, the tension was palpable, especially when terrorism or the security forces was involved. I well recall conducting the funeral of one of the victims of the Chinook helicopter disaster in which 29 people including some of Northern Ireland's top security and intelligence personnel tragically perished. I always had to be very careful what I said on these occasions.

****

Funerals were not always a positive show of respect and support. I remember the horrific TV news footage from March 1988, when the two British soldiers dressed in civilian clothes were dragged from their unmarked car, stripped and brutally beaten and shot dead by a mob as they drove into an IRA funeral procession. This happened just weeks before our first visit and was still very fresh in our minds and the public mind at the time I came home to Angela from a meeting with my College Principal and asked her how she would feel about a summer pastorate in Belfast. Our family and friends thought we were quite mad, especially as they knew we could consider a similar pastorate in a nice, quiet, middle class and civilised place like Horsham, in Sussex; a nice thought, but not for me.

The killing of the two soldiers was part of a terrible sequence of events, a chain reaction, sadly not uncommon in the Province, where one atrocity could be followed by a reprisal, sparking another tit-for-tat killing; a growing cycle of violence.

I recall going on what was called the Revolutionary Tour of West Belfast, including Milltown cemetery with its infamous IRA section, this before peace was settled and considered a foolhardy and dangerous visit by many in my community. I remember standing at the graveside of the three members of the IRA said by the inscription on the gravestone to have been, "Murdered by the British on Gibraltar." The deaths in Gibraltar had been the subject of ITV's *Death on the Rock* documentary, investigating claims of a shoot to kill policy by the British Government. This was part of a horrific series of connected events. Close by was another headstone remembering those who had been killed at that very funeral, when Protestant Michael Stone carried out a revenge attack on the mourners at the very spot; yes, murder at the graveside, during a funeral. A press report marking the 20th anniversary of these events read:

Twenty years ago a lethal chain of events began in Gibraltar that ended 13 days later in Belfast with eight people dead and 68 injured. It was one of the most vicious periods in the Northern Ireland conflict and none of three protagonists- Britain, Irish republicans, and Ulster loyalists emerged with any credit. Briefly, this is what happened. On March 6 in Gibraltar, SAS troops shot dead Dan McCann, Seán Savage and Mairéad Farrell, who were all members of an IRA active service unit. On March 16 at their funeral in Milltown cemetery, Belfast, a loyalist gunman, Michael Stone, fired shots and lobbed grenades into the crowd, killing three and wounding many others. On March 19 at the same cemetery, the crowd attending the burial of Kevin Brady, one of Stone's victims, hauled two out-of-uniform British corporals, Derek Woods and David Howes, from their car. The two were then stripped naked, beaten, and finally shot dead by the IRA.

Even funerals, it seemed, were not sacrosanct or immune from terrorist activities in those times.

I also recall being very surprised by my fellow clerics' advice not to attend as a supportive gesture the funerals of the innocent members of the nearby Loughinisland community, who had been mercilessly gunned down by paramilitaries whilst watching on TV the Republic of Ireland football team play Italy in the 1994 World Cup finals. Again this was part of a chain of terrible events:

On 16 June 1994, the Irish National Liberation Army (INLA) shot dead three Ulster Volunteer Force (UVF) members on the Shankill Road

44

in Belfast. The following day, the UVF launched two "revenge attacks." In the first, UVF members shot dead a Catholic civilian taxi driver in Carrickfergus, in the second, they shot dead two Protestant civilians in Newtownabbey, whom they assumed were Catholics. The Loughinisland massacre, a day later, is believed to have been a further "revenge attack." On the evening of 18 June 1994, about 24 people were gathered in The Heights Bar watching the Republic of Ireland v ItalyWorld Cup soccer match. At 10:10pm, two UVF members armed with assault rifles walked into the pub and opened fire on the crowd. Six men were killed outright.

I did meet some of the survivors of this horrific incident in my role as Chaplain to the local hospital, and we clerics did go to the parish Priest on the night before the funerals to offer our support and prayers.

Fainting at the funeral and calling at a rather difficult time

Other funerals come to mind. I remember what I can only describe as a very rough and tough family. They might well have been described as travellers. They turned up at the manse one day, well, three or four male representatives of the family, claiming an ancient allegiance to the church, requesting that I conduct the funeral of a family member at the local crematorium and cemetery, Roselawn. I was always happy to perform such a service and readily agreed. As I have said they were a rather rough family, a little dishevelled, battered even, by the hardships of life if not by adversaries, or perhaps both, and more than a little menacing. I met with them a number of times and they were quite demanding and exacting in what they wanted as part of the funeral. As always I spent a good number of hours preparing for it. "We will pay your usual fee," they assured me. "We have had a whip round and we have it all ready for you." Now, I was never troubled about the customary fee paid to ministers and to the church by non-church members for such services. I was always more than happy to help and a fee was never a big issue for me. I did appreciate that they had the decency to recognize that they were requesting a service which took time and money to provide.

The day came and I diligently carried out my duties. First, there was a service in the church, then a shorter service at the graveside. There was a huge number of mourners, with scores and scores of close family members, some of whom had prepared for the ordeal by taking some "Dutch courage" and plenty of it in some cases. The atmosphere was intense. Emotions were high. I led the coffin from the hearse to the graveside and stood and faced the multitude who gathered around and before me. I began to speak. Then I heard a thud as one of the family standing to one side of and slightly behind me, just out of my sight, fainted. Then another thud, as another mourner fainted. It was pandemonium. The two women who were overcome either by the emotion of the occasion or the alcoholic fumes which enveloped us all, or both, were being dragged up off the ground onto their feet by their relatives. People were flapping around them, literally flapping at them with scarves, hats and newspapers, trying to revive them.

My immediate thought was what should I do? This could quickly turn into a farce. I was mindful that it was a very solemn occasion and that everything had to be done with the greatest of reverence and respect. Moreover, I was in charge. At these times it was my stage. I was manager and director of proceedings. I was responsible. I could stop and wait, but for how long? Or I could carry on as best I could with as much dignity I could muster? All of this and more went flashing through my mind. I was also very aware of the pressure on the undertaker, who invariably had other funerals to service and a very tight schedule, as did the cemetery staff.

I decided to carry on. "If you can keep your head when all about you are losing theirs," wrote Kipling. I did my best to keep mine. I carried on with what I hoped was dignity and completed the interment.

The family were very, very grateful and warmly thanked me for the service and my words of comfort. The two ladies made a good recovery. The eldest son shook my hand and said,"Thank you so much Reverend. You did us proud." He clutched my hand, stared at me intently and added, "I will be in to see you soon with the money, we have it all collected up from 'em all. They've all given."

His parting words were meant to be reassuring, "I will be in to see you with it soon."

Nearly twenty-five years later, I am still waiting.

****

Perhaps the biggest surprise of all, which captures beautifully the huge difference in attitudes between England and Northern Ireland at the time, occurred a few years later, a few weeks after we returned home from Northern Ireland to minister to a congregation in Lancashire. In Northern Ireland then everyone it seemed had some connection to a church. Even if church attendance was slowly declining it was still massively higher than in England, and most families would preserve their

48

historic links to a church and pay in their annual membership fee. The Stipend, as it was called, was paid to the church to ensure the services of the minister, the right of burial in the graveyard in the family plot and to maintain the links to the church in which generations of the family had been Christened, married or buried, or "hatched, matched and dispatched," as it was flippantly referred to by some of my colleagues.

Back in England church membership and attendance was thin in comparison. Christianity in England, according to my narrow snapshot, by then played a very minor and peripheral role in social life. In Northern Ireland it was still a major force. I often felt very uncomfortable at the reaction of people, even complete strangers, to my clerical collar. Some, perhaps upwards of fifty years my senior, would call me "Father." Others, even once a complete stranger in a queue in a bank, felt the need to "confess" to me as to why they had not been to their own church for a while, and this includes the eminent and lofty Consultant Obstetrician who delivered our son Andy to the sound of machine gunfire on the anniversary of the death of the IRA hunger striker, Bobby Sands, in August of 1991.

The office of ministry was greatly respected in Northern Ireland, perhaps even feared by some, and its visible symbol, the clerical collar, certainly had a powerful effect on many. Once, a shopkeeper reduced my £25 pair of shoes to £20 because of the collar in spite of my protests. It opened many doors. I was often waived straight through police and Army road blocks and check points, often saluted on my

49

way, thus saving me considerable time, and I am sure that it was only because of my collar that I was invited to be present at Andy's birth by caesarean section in the Royal Victoria Hospital. I was scrubbed up and gowned, booted and capped in green. I saw the whole thing from start to finish. The consultant even told his staff to move up around the operating table to make room for me. This was a real privilege, if not for the squeamish.

On the contrary, often, back in England, I was made to feel the minister was an outdated eccentric, to be humoured, tolerated or pitied, even. The difference in the two situations was made crystal clear when a familiar call came from a senior member of my new English congregation, "There has been a death."

The call was to inform me of the death of an elderly lady who had some historical links to my new congregation. There was every chance that I would be asked to conduct the funeral. I went straight into gear. No naive, green, partly trained minister this time. I was well and truly trained and blooded after years of formal training and five years of extensive pastoral experience in Northern Ireland, plus the several vacation pastorates. I knew what to do. This time I was in charge. I drove the few miles to the house, parked up and knocked on the door. Granted I was collarless. (I had never been really comfortable with the very visible way of setting one apart and had discarded it on our return to England). I did make sure the lady who answered the door knew who I was. After all, I did not want to cause her any additional concern. I was a complete stranger and it was a difficult time.

"Good morning," I said, and to identify myself added, "I am Reverend Rowley of Nazarene Chapel."

"Oh dear," the lady replied. She paused and then added, "You have called at a rather difficult time. There has been a death in the family. Could you come back another time?"

Home visits: much tea, many cakes, bowls of jelly and broken crockery

Crash! A sinking feeling came over Angela and me, and our blood chilled as a shocked silence descended upon the room. For a moment or two, it seemed like several, no one moved. Then one of the two elderly sisters made her way to the kitchen. Fearing the worst, we all got up and followed her. We were right.

It was not the girls' fault. After all, who would serve afternoon tea to two young children in a 150 year old, irreplaceable tea service, which had been bought abroad many, many years ago by the paternal grandfather on one of his seafaring travels? Well, the two sisters did just that, wanting to do full justice to the honour of the visit of the minister and his family, they warmly welcomed us into their very large ancestral home, which stood imposingly on the shore of Strangford Loch, some twenty-five miles south-east of Belfast, and served high-tea to us using this priceless antique tea set. The house was beautiful, if somewhat faded, and every corner of each of the pine-walled rooms was filled with oil paintings, clocks and other antiques, every artefact holding memories from long ago, each with its own story to tell – a travelogue of exotic places. The sisters, now in their very late 80s, had lived together since the death of the elder's husband two years before, a funeral I had shared in during one of our summer visits. The other sister had never married, and now the two were re-united in the family home, which had not seen or heard children for many decades.

It wasn't the girls' fault; we could not really blame them, could we? After all they were only about seven and three years old, or so. No one could know what would happen, although looking back today we might have guessed; but it was only afternoon tea. What could go wrong?

****

Tea never meant just tea, of course. "Have a wee drop of tea" actually meant have as many cups of tea as your bladder could bear and at least several rounds of sandwiches and cakes and biscuits a plenty, "Just to keep you going until dinner time." A cup of tea never meant just a cup of tea. Mrs Doyle in *Father Ted* is not a completely fictional character, I can assure you. We met many such characters. The hospitality shown to us was immense and food featured large during our time in Northern Ireland. This was clear from our very first visit when we were introduced to the Ulster Fry, an impressive challenge of a fry-up, which was probably responsible for the much repeated tale that Northern Ireland had the worst heart attack record in Europe, one repeated often enough to convince us although we are still not sure as to the substance and statistics behind the claim. But it was the manner in which this was shared which interested us, it was almost a boast.

Whilst we could never look at a Fry without thinking of all of the oil sticking onto unseen tubes and blocked arteries, we did acquire a taste for the soda, potato and wheaten breads which went with it. Most of the Fry was off limits to us, of course, as we were strict vegetarians. This fact, too, set us apart rather in a predominately farming community. I am not sure that the concept of vegetarianism had reached Ulster twenty-five years ago, from either a health perspective or out of a compassion for animals.

Strange and strained were the occasional conversations connected to animal welfare we shared or overheard: the story of the 6,000 battery hens farmed by one member of the congregation; how Sammy kindly and matter-of-factly offered in our hearing to shoot his neighbour's goat for him when it was beyond use; how another had left his farm dog outside overnight with a badly cut paw to find in the morning it had bled to death. Vets were expensive, of course, but we hoped it was an accident or oversight rather than the mean streak in him suggested to us by a cousin of his, who had many years before fallen out with him over a family will and had never spoken to him again. Surely he would not have done such a thing to save a few pounds? But we could not be sure. After all, this was the same man who forever bemoaned the financial lot of the farmers, constantly whined on about diminishing Milk Quotas and always equated any consideration of my annual Stipend (salary) rise and, indeed, any expenditure from the church account to the downturn over the years in the price of cabbages per sack at market.

This was the same man who would never allow anyone to throw out anything belonging to the church, for nothing was deemed by him to be too old or trivial to be beyond storage. From the smallest off-cuts of wood, old carpets or bales of wire to huge and unwieldy old doors, sheets of glass, odd bricks and old sacks; it was all stored in the very large building which stood next to the manse and served as a double garage. The rumour was it had served as a stable in days gone by. The problem now was it was filled to capacity with so much old junk that we could barely walk into it let alone park a car in it. My repeated requests at committee meetings to allow me to have a good clear out of this old clutter were always met with strong resistance by this one character, for "You never know when it might come in handy," and "This would cost a lot, you know." Others were not the same and quietly suggested that I clear out what I did not want on a day when the man in question was out at market and they would come by the stealth of night with a trailer and take it all away to be burnt, never to be seen again. When I asked if this would be ok, they replied, "By the time he realizes it has gone it will be too late."

After several hours of hard work, and a few late-evening trips under the cover of darkness by a farmer with his trailer, we were able to park our car in the garage. The deed was never discovered.

Generally, issues of animal welfare and vegetarianism were conveniently left aside for everyone's sake and sensibilities. We did not want to invite trouble. After all this was a farming community and we had to respect ways which were foreign to us. Little did we know that trouble was not far from coming to us and not over the issue of animal rights.

We did sit through one farm lunch, when all the men and women were in from the fields, horrified as the man of the house discussed and explained to a neighbour with great gusto and in great and gory detail to all assembled the various ways to "home slaughter" a cow and what to do with the carcass. The details I would not like to repeat here. It was not for the faint-hearted, and especially not for vegetarians.

This was the same house where much baking was done for church events. Every church function, be it bowls night, committee meetings, fundraising events, business, social, spiritual or pleasure, all were accompanied by huge quantities of food, following an afternoon of intense preparation and baking by the ladies of the congregation. Sandwiches, salads, pickles and coleslaws strained the legs of many a table. The puddings and cakes, the sweet things, freshly baked with military precision at home, "traybakes," as they were called, and brought up to the church just before the event by the ladies of the church's Women's

League: dozens and dozens, carloads, of "buns," or cakes or pastries as we knew them, of all types: flapjacks, shortbread, apple tarts, lemon curd tarts, strawberry tarts, chocolate caramels and all manner of gateaux, and more. And the king of the sweets, seemingly a national or at least regional dish and subject of great pride, a source even of competition as to who could produce the best, the lightest, the fluffiest, pavlova: huge mounds of sweet rock which exploded into powder as you bit into it and then descended into a chewy, gooey, glue like residue which adhered to teeth like tile adhesive. All accompanied by lashings of whipped or double cream, or both.

****

It was the same house, and at the same lunch, where we were inducted into the fineries of slaughtering and butchering a cow, that we sat and watched the lady of the house remove the baby's nappy, march over to the sink, which was half-filled with soaking crockery left over from breakfast, and dunk the baby's bare and encrusted bottom into the same sink and water, skilfully manoeuvring it in and out and around the plates, mugs, tea cups and saucers. She then, without breaking off from conversation, or disturbing the rhythm of her obviously well practised routine, slickly dried the baby's bottom with the tea towel found on the side of the sink draining board, replaced the tea towel for further use, and placed baby on the floor, all in one movement. We at best only sort of picked over our sandwiches and buns after seeing this.

****

This was not the only experience of what shall I say were less than hygienic ways. Gurtie was a sweet old lady. No one knew exactly how old she was, but she must have been at least 90. She lived around the corner from the church in one of the executive homes. When we were first told about the village estate consisting of these executive homes we had visions of some swish maisonettes or large detached homes, the sort found in Essex housing the commuters who lived along the Central Line. How wrong we were. They were what we would call council houses, and very small, cheap, grey, very grey, prefab type accommodation.

Gurtie had lived in hers for many years. It looked as if she had never actually cleaned it, bless her. She was a contented soul, if rather eccentric, and very, very hospitable to callers. My, was she hospitable to callers. Never a cup of tea though, unusual though this was for these parts, but, and I was forewarned that this would be the case but never quite believed it, a big bowl of jelly. Yes, jelly. Whether it was in the height of summer or the freezing depths of winter with four inches of snow on the ground, Gurtie presented every visitor with a big bowl of jelly. "This will do you good," she would declare as she thrust it and a dubious looking spoon into my hand, the latter looking like it was still covered with the remains of a previous caller's treat, and ushered me to sit at the table. Well I think it was a table as it was covered and concealed by a multitude of old newspapers, half-empty cans of food, items of clothing and so on and a huge bowl of jelly – the mother bowl – looking decidedly furry, with white and green mould in places. Gurtie might have been eccentric, but how she enjoyed the regular visits from the new young minister, so much so that on one occasion she honoured me with a second bowl of jelly, a rare treat, indeed.

I would often contemplate ways of concealing the jelly when she was not looking, I even thought of perhaps slipping it into my pocket in order to take it outside and dispose of it later. But Gurtie had eagle eyes and never looked away. I thought of trying to convince her that I was allergic to it, but decided I could not carry it off, and I could not bring myself to lie to her, even when part of me began to suspect that this ritual was carried out with just a hint of devilment. So what did I do each time? I did what all young, new and enthusiastic ministers would have done, I gingerly made my way through each spoonful, often nearly gagging as the ice-cold slime reached the back of my throat. What else could I do? I wouldn't have hurt her feelings for the world. And I was not the only one who received this treatment.

One of my Elders, whose role was to supplement the minister's visiting, had forewarned me about the jelly ritual, but I had not taken him seriously. This gentleman, who was the most genuine, kindly, if fastidious, of individuals, eventually told me that he had a technique for surviving the event, as he put it. Brian, a dapper man who had a high-powered job in the City of Belfast, said he was always prepared for his visits to Gurtie's home. He made sure that he had a bottle of brandy in his car and as soon as he had left her house he took two large swigs from it. This, he said, not only killed the taste of the jelly, but probably killed off any germs picked up in the process.

****

Immediately following the visit to the two elderly sisters for high-tea served in the antique china tea service, both Angela and I needed a stiff drink to calm our nerves. We were both in a state of shock for some time. But, it wasn't the girls' fault. They were just being helpful.

All four of us adults had agreed how nice it was when Alex offered to help clear away the tea cups, saucers, plates and the silver cutlery. And Faith wanted to help. How sweet they looked as they stacked the used china on to the tea trolley. How cute and angelic they looked as they gently pushed the trolley towards the kitchen and out of sight. "What lovely girls," both sisters readily agreed. "How proud you…" Then, crash. A terrible sound came from the direction of the kitchen, the sound of smashing china.

In the car on the way home, Alex and Faith, to break the deafening silence, tried to explain what had happened. They were simply trying to push the trolley over the small ridge between the hall and the kitchen, and one or other of them, or both, although both denied it, pushed a little too hard and the trolley tipped over, spilling its load of irreplaceable, valuable china, with its huge sentimental value, on to the hard wooden floor.

When we moved in response to the crash, initially we were all frozen to the spot, as still as Lot's wife, and then reached the scene of the accident; the sight which met us was not a good one. Now of course the most important thing was that neither of the girls was hurt. This aside, the image of the upside down trolley, and the two bemused little girls, whose faces were returning from a shocked white now to blush bright crimson, standing surrounded by broken bits of cups and saucers and plates, is as clear today as the day it happened twenty-five years ago.

In all about a dozen pieces were broken. Beyond repair? Of course they were. "We are so sorry we said," many times. "Can we possible replace these pieces?" Both sisters seemed somewhat dazed. They did not actually speak, rather they nodded to accept the apology, or so we hoped, and then shook their heads in unison, "No," these pieces could not be replaced. Not much more was said on that occasion and after a polite pause we felt the best thing to do was to make a discrete departure for home.

My, did we need a stiff drink by the time we got there. In comparison, Brian's two swigs of brandy to survive his jelly ordeal was nothing.

****

Later that evening I telephoned the sisters to ask how they were. By then they had recovered some of their composure and generously said it was an accident and it could not be helped. I visited the house a good number of times after the saga of the broken crockery. They never referred to it again. And we were never again invited to tea there as a family.

Visits to the manse, a very cold manse, very slowly turning pink

When I got into the habit of describing the manse as a goldfish bowl I was not exaggerating; it was true. We had almost no privacy at all. At almost any time of day or night a caller or callers would appear unannounced; we were expected to let them in and I was expected to spend quality time with them, offering tea as well as comfort. Of course, if there was a real emergency I did not mind in the least. It was part of my job and calling. I was there to support and serve at some of life's toughest times: a death, an illness, a marriage breakdown or very serious family rows and fallouts. I would not have had it any other way. However, some callers were simply dropping in to be friendly, or worse, in some cases to be nosey. I remember once looking out from my study at the front of the house as two church members, walking arm-in-arm along the footpath the other side of the manse's fairly extensive front garden, and peering in so hard through the bay window, in order to see who was inside talking to me, that they walked straight into the lamp-post. Our windows were now exposed as we had thrown out the dirty, grey net curtains which had afforded some protection and privacy.

I recall two weeks I took as a "holiday" after we had been in situ for a few months. My intention was to use this time to decorate the manse from top to bottom to cheer it and us up. It was quite a depressing house really. It stood imposingly large and grand, with its double frontage and five bedrooms; a symbol of power and presence in this rural setting. But to us it was a barracks and we could never get it warm. It was really cold, both in character and temperature. Its grey paint on the outside suited it well. As I have already mentioned the weather in Northern Ireland was not kind, and the manse stood backing onto wide open fields and the cold, fierce wind cut through it like a knife. The large and cavernous hall leading to the grand stairway would immediately fill with a rush of cold air whenever a door, back or front, was opened, which happened a lot to let callers in or out. We could almost see the temperature drop and register its demise by the steam forming on our breaths. It was impossible to get it warm; and the primary source of heating was an economy-seven system.

****

I am not sure who thought up the idea of economy-seven storage heaters. We had never encountered these before. I understood from the congregation that the idea was to heat up the bricks inside at night when electricity was at its cheapest, and the stored heat was then dispersed to order during the day. Some hope! Perhaps our system was very old, or in need of repair, but it was awful. We charged it up all night ok, but after just an hour or two of a minimum seepage of marginal warmth, that was it; it was over, all by about 10.00am. No more heat would be forthcoming from these radiators until they had been through the same ritual the next night. Twelve hours of charging at the cheap rate, and very little output next day. The little heat which was emitted was instantly lost in the large, damp, rooms and huge hallway. We never did get used to the lack of heating in the manse. It was always unpleasant. And it was not that we were soft and used to all modern creature comforts, not at all. Both Angela and I had been born in poor, inner London and had clear memories of outside toilets, no proper bath and the only heating being a coal fire. I have strangely fond memories of my grandfather disappearing down into the depths of his coal cellar, which could be accessed only by the door from the living room of his two-up-two-down rented house, only to appear a few minutes later, this when the coal was low and in need of replenishing, triumphant and sooty with a bucket containing the remnants of the week's delivery found at the bottom of the pitch-black coal cellar.

****

We were not that soft, or so we thought. But the manse seemed to bring hard living to a new level. Perhaps we had changed over the years and softened; whatever, try as we might, we could not get the manse warm. We did try, but on a very limited income it was impossible to do more than keep a coal fire burning in one of the two front rooms and

65

adopt this as the main room of the house. At least this gave us a chance of thawing out whenever we returned home. This meant there was a great reluctance in all of us to leave this room and make our way upstairs to the toilet or to bed. Especially as when we opened the door all of the heat generated by the coal, we burnt lots of it even to maintain this lowly comfort, was sucked out to be lost in the freezing hall.

So, the manse was always freezing, in spite of our best efforts. This was especially true of the kitchen. It was very large and tiled from floor to ceiling, and it seemed to hold the chill of the Northern Irish weather much better than the storage heaters held the warmth of their night time charge. Found at the back of the house and exposed to the driving winds which howled through the back door, heated by one economy-seven storage heater and whatever heat came from cooking, it was not a pleasant place to be. I can still picture Angela standing over the small, electric, oil-filled radiator we added, with one leg either side of it, allowing the hot air to rise up her skirt. This was one method she devised for getting warm. The other was to keep with her a hot water bottle and constantly refill it as soon as its temperature began to drop. It remained strapped to her for hours at a time.

When we mentioned to the congregation how difficult it was to heat such a large and rambling house, we received some sympathy. Heather, for example, brought us a gas cylinder heater she no longer required, a wonderful gesture, except it too proved very costly, certainly on top of the coal and electricity. It, too, fought a losing battle, lost in the vast cold space of the manse, and it left behind both fumes and condensation. It was a very kind thought, though. A kindness much appreciated. It was certainly a contrast to the response from one elderly lady, the daughter of a former neighbouring minister who had long since died. She had visited and stayed in this very manse on many occasions as a child many, many years ago. "You are lucky," she said, "we didn't have them storage heaters then and there was a great big hole in the back door. And we had a rat which came in and out of it into the kitchen larder."

My, how lucky we felt: no longer was there a hole in the back door, and the rat we assumed was long gone.

****

On my many home visits, most of which were to very modest homes and many very small, two-up-two-down dwellings, it was a great contrast to the situation at home to walk into a small, cosy front room where all the family gathered around the roaring fire, squashed on to a couple of sofas and the odd chair here and there. A place was always made for the minister right in front of the fire, and more coal or wood was added to it. At times the heat in such a small area was overwhelming. What a lovely problem to have I often thought, being too hot; one easily remedied by opening a window for a few moments to let in a blast of the Northern Irish night air. That soon did the trick and cooled things down, until the next bucket of coal was thrown on to start the process once more. Then, for me, it was out into the night air and on to another house, another visit, at times until after midnight, then home to the cold manse.

****

The manse had not been decorated for many years. To put it kindly, it had seen much better days; outside it was grey, prison-block grey, as were most of the church buildings and the executive homes in Moneymore. Inside, it was brown. It was very brown: brown walls and paintwork, and brown carpets. It had been hastily furnished for us with a multitude of cast offs. This was a kind gesture for our first pastorate, after which much of the furniture was removed and taken back to the donors. We were not too sorry to see most of it go as the strange array of odd furniture made the place look like the inside of something I was to see in Romania a bit later on. It was then left to us to bring what furniture we had from England and to buy lots of essentials at auction in Belfast, in an attempt to fill up this huge place on the cheap and make it reasonably habitable.

We also had to do something about the depressing decorations. However, my attempt to decorate the manse, to brighten it up during a two-week holiday, did not go according to plan. Looking back it was quite farcical. There I was on the first day of my holiday, up early preparing to start painting, hoping to get in a good day's work. I had all the materials, newly bought filler, brushes, turps and paint, both gloss and emulsion. So fed up of the dark brown walls and lighter brown paint in the manse, which gave it a dark, sombre and depressing feel, we had decided in a reactionary moment of madness to go for bright pink woodwork and lighter pink walls. It was to be very pink indeed, a terrific contrast to the brown of many years. It certainly brightened up the place. In retrospect it was, perhaps, a little too much, and it certainly proved to be a shock to the visiting congregation when it was eventually finished. And that was the problem, getting it finished.

I had cleared Angela and the children out of the house on a trip to the seaside, locked the dog in the front room, put down the dust sheets and stirred the paint. I then went up the ladder. The day before I had borrowed the ancient set of ladders from the church store and brought it into the manse. This set seemed to be a very much homemade affair, consisting of two extremely long ladders hinged together at the top. Tatty rope stopped the two ladders from splaying out too far and collapsing. There were a couple of rungs missing and one or two looked like they were about to follow. All in all, it looked none too safe, and I was a more than a little dubious about using it, especially as I knew I would have to go right to the very top to reach the far corners and recesses of the hall ceiling. But as I knew it was still used in the church to change light bulbs in the most inaccessible of places, I pressed on. After all, I had not heard of it giving way, and I was sure that if it was really unsafe the committee would not have begrudged spending a few pounds on a nice new and safe replacement set. Today I wonder?

This set was now open and standing precariously in the cavernous hall. Up I went, clutching paint pot and brush. I waited for the ladders to steady, and I was about to put the first splash of colour on the wall, right at the top of this set of very long and rickety ladders, when there was a knock on the front door.

I came down the ladders, carefully put down the tin of paint and the brush, and opened the front door. There on the doorstep was Mrs Grounds, a very sweet elderly lady. "I have just called to see how you are. You are on holiday aren't you? That must be nice for you and the family?" She proceeded to walk in and then accepted my invite into the front room, where she sat and chatted for more than an hour, telling me of the local news and her aches and pains. After I stood and watched her go up the path and shut the door, I tried again. Up the ladder, paint pot in hand and knock, knock. It was another visitor. Another congregant who just wanted to tell me that Mrs Mcilroy had been taken into hospital. "I know you are on holiday, but I thought you would want to know," she said, leaving me with a bit of a dilemma: should I go and visit Mrs Mcilroy or not? Well, I thought, I suppose a quick drive into the hospital later wouldn't hurt.

And so it went on. Next was Miss Potten with some pancakes she had made for us and a little wheaten bread

70

for our "teas," then a visitor to ask about a wedding, and later, with me by this time covered in paint splashes and not so much on the walls or woodwork, one about a funeral, then a delivery of coal from the coalman, also a member of the congregation. He, too, wanted to chat. Such was the pace of life in the Province. There was always time for a chat; a very nice way of life if you had the time to enjoy it. But not when there was a very large manse to paint. Next it was the gravediggers who wanted the key to the shed where the church lawnmowers were kept, then the community policemen, who always liked to call by and have a drop of tea, keep me informed of local events and to see if I had anything to share with them. They were imposing figures, complete with their flak jackets and handguns, and their automatic rifles very visible. And so it went on. The first two or three days passed and I got little done to transform the manse from a brown monstrosity into a pink palace of which Barbara Cartland would have been proud.

There was only one thing for it. I received my callers during the day and started work on the painting at about ten o'clock each evening when the children were in bed and the house relatively quiet. I worked on through the night to three or four o'clock in the morning. It was hard going, but it was the only way to get the job done. A week later the pink carpet we had ordered from a Belfast carpet warehouse arrived and was fitted to complete the transformation. We were very pleased with it. At least it was bright and cheery. We did wonder if it was a bit bright.

The transformation did bring some odd looks from our visitors for quite a while. The only comment we got was from a very prominent and senior member of the congregation. As she stood there in the hall with arms folded and shaking her head from side to side, a look and a shake we were to see again in the future more than once, she simply said, "Oh, you've gone for pink then."

More home visits: two tangerines and a banana, the Zen art of knocking without knocking, and the barn which wasn't there

Much of my work outside of Sunday services involved visiting my congregation in their homes. Richard Baxter, the 17th century English non-conformist church leader and preacher, said the minister must be a visiting minister. It was said that he was always visiting from "house to house." So, it was his fault, then.

How literally this was taken by my congregation in this very traditional region of Ulster where I was minister. The people did not always come to church, but the minister was expected to take the church to them, whether they liked it or not. Many who rarely showed up at church but wanted to stay in the fold, paid the annual membership fee, the Stipend, for family reasons and to preserve their roots. This enabled them to have the services of a minister on call, just in case. They would often offer sincere and polite apologies for why they had not been to a service for such a long time, and, with grave sincerity, promise to come along that very next Sunday, a promise rarely fulfilled. I imagine now some of the younger generations would not be quite so accommodating. Then, whatever time of day or night I called, I was warmly welcomed in and given a seat by the fire.

There was always a huge coal or log fire burning, even in the summer time. Ulster weather was not moderate. It was often cold and damp. So to pass time sitting by the fire and chatting to the good families of my congregation was a nice experience, but it did take up time. If it was around a meal time a chair was drawn up by the table and a plate set, unless my protests were strong and loud. If it was not near a meal time it would be at least a cup of tea and a plate of buns, cakes and fruit loaf. It was said that the rent man was kept on the doorstep; the policeman required a warrant and the doctor an invite, but the minister was always welcomed in at any time of day or night. Getting in was never a problem. Getting out was rather more difficult.

****

For me it was a delight to visit those who I felt really needed it, those in residential homes, or nursing homes; those who rarely got out of their own home because of ill-health or old age; those who were bereft or going through immense problems. Then every second of the time spent was a privilege and a joy. However, I could never understand the need to visit every member of the congregation twice a year with the Communion Card. This was exactly what it sounds like: a small, white visiting card which was to be presented to each congregant in time to announce the biannual Service of Holy Communion. My job was to visit everyone to rally the troops for what were to some the two most important services of the year. I could not understand the reasoning behind it. My life was extremely busy looking after the day-to-day concerns of a large congregation, with scores of hospital and home visits, numerous meetings, preparing weekly and occasional services and all the rich variety of the minister's lot in such a traditional and demanding situation. My working life was relentless.

One week I started counting up my working hours from the first Sunday morning service to the end of a long committee meeting long, long past midnight on the Tuesday. At that point I had clocked up over 45 hours and the week was still young. Days off did not feature. On top of this my congregation was spread, with members living far and wide, with a concentration in the villages and towns outside of Belfast, and odd members living 20,30 even 40 miles away to the north and south of the city.

Looking back it is no wonder that I found communion visits a strange affair and not the best use of time. To visit over 200 homes in about six weeks leading up to the special service was no mean feat, a feat I had managed to achieve during our very first summer pastorate, a feat which impressed my potential future congregation no end. If lucky I would catch people home, if they were out then the expectation was that I would make return visits until I did catch them in. It seemed a ridiculous use of my time. And, to add insult to injury I had to pay for the petrol, this on a very meagre Stipend.

I did make every effort to try to fulfil this requirement for at least two or three cycles, but in the end I spoke out and said I felt this was not really necessary or to the benefit of the people of the church. My words did not go down well. After all, my predecessor had done it and his before him. I was told that one not so many decades ago made his visits on horseback and stabled his horse in what was now my garage. For one horrible moment I had the awful feeling that they were going to suggest I should do the same. Fortunately, no one did.

****

It was a similar issue following the harvest services and taking out the harvest goods. Being predominantly, at least historically, a farming congregation, with many prominent members still working on the land, the harvest service was well attended and richly supported in terms of goods donated. It was always a source of great pride that their church harvest display was the best in the area. The work started the Saturday before when the team arrived to dress the church. All day long people arrived bearing goods. Crates of cabbages, sacks and sacks of potatoes and carrots, and huge quantities of anything you can think of to do with harvest. Milk churns full of milk straight from the cow, slabs of cheese and butter, dozens of eggs and centre of stage a large work of art, made from bread baked in the shape of a sheaf of wheat. And there were flowers enough to widen a florist's eyes. The church always looked wonderful. It was a long, hard day dressing it and not always the happiest band of helpers who did it. At times the Christian spirit was in short supply. There were often squabbles over the displays and who was to do what, and who had brought the most or least. On one occasion, soon after our arrival, we were told to watch Mrs B………. as it had been known for things to go missing from handbags when she was around.

Worst of all was the Monday following the Sunday services and the ritual of distributing the harvest gifts. Following the long, hard work of Saturday dressing the church and the inevitable two services at my own church, and one or two elsewhere on the Sunday, Monday morning arrived and with it a smaller team arrived at the church very early to begin to take the display apart and wrap up the goods in small bags for distribution. Distribute to whom? Well, the flowers were more often or not taken to the local residential homes, hospitals and hospices, which I thought was a lovely idea. They were always very warmly received and gave a lot of pleasure to many. The large, resplendent displays worthy of any flower show brightened up the darkest of receptions, including at the local hospices and hospitals. The vegetables, fruit, tins and packets were to be taken out to the elderly members of the congregation. This took a huge amount of time and the senselessness of some of this was never more apparent to me than when on the trip to the far reaches of Bangor to see Mr Macmillan.

My church officers bagged up the various produce early on the Monday morning, themselves removing a few token items to take out to members of the congregation who lived near to them, and then gave me a long list of those who were to receive goods, pointing to the small mountain of little brown bags containing just an apple and an orange, or so. "This one is for Mr X and this for Mrs Y," and then Mr Macmillan's, a bag containing two tangerines and a banana.

A very nice thought it seemed, but Mr Macmillan lived about 38 miles away, had not set foot in the church for years and he was stone-deaf and never heard the front doorbell. I would end up banging on his door for 15 or 20 minutes, wandering around the house, up the back drive and peering through windows to try to raise him in order to present him with two or three pieces of fruit, which by now, very late on Monday, or even Tuesday morning, after hanging around from early Saturday, purchased perhaps on the Friday, or even Thursday before, looked decidedly worse for wear. I would end up leaving the small brown bag of fruit on his doorstep, this involving a 76 mile round trip and 2 or 3 gallons of petrol that we could barely afford.

In the course of several annual attempts during our time in Northern Ireland, undertaken partly out of stoic determination, and in a vain effort to maintain the greatly valued traditions no matter how unreasonable they seemed to me and so to please the congregation, I never once managed to hand the goods over to Mr Macmillan in person. The best I managed was only a polite chat to his niece over the telephone later that day, after the gift was discovered by her as she visited her uncle. They, she assured me, were always very grateful, and she was profuse in expressing their gratitude.

****

Given the huge amount of visiting I had to do to look after the spiritual needs of the sick, lonely, elderly and those with problems, it is perhaps no wonder that I felt pretty ground down and more than a little used by some of the less reasonable demands of my congregation. So, I came up with a strategy, a strategy born of desperation and the need to survive. I have to confess that during some of the communion visits mentioned above, when I had 200 plus home visits to make, on top of the day-to-day demands of a large congregation, a strategy evolved. This I hasten to add was only for some of the homes, the homes of those who I had seen very regularly and very recently at church and church events, those who I knew would want no more than to catch up on the news, gossip even, of the church and especially those who would perhaps tolerate me and fulfil their obligation by engaging me in small talk for an hour or so and in the process make great and empty promises about future church attendance.

I now look back and call the strategy the Zen art of knocking without knocking. I stress that I would never have done this at homes where there was a genuine need, but on a good number of occasions, times when I was under so much pressure to visit everyone in the six-week period leading up to the special service, I was able to knock so quietly and slip the Communion Card so gently through the letterbox that those inside never heard me. I could see the shapes and shadows behind the curtained lounge and hear the television blaring out loudly, and I, with the stealth, grace and poise of an SAS commando, was able to leave my calling card and be on my way. Sometimes this involved stooping low to avoid being seen through a window. What a result it was when I could tick the box and get on my way to the next house on my list, enabled to report back to my next Church Committee meeting that I had delivered cards to 45 houses since the last meeting. It truly was, at times, the art of knocking without knocking.

****

Some of the most difficult of all the home visits I carried out occurred during the very first summer experience, when, partly to welcome us and partly I am sure to impress us sufficiently in order for me to return to minister on a permanent basis, I was encouraged to visit all of the members of the congregation, over 200 homes. Church officers and members took me to many of these, and at times the whole family was invited for tea, but much of this visiting was carried out on my own, often causing me to get lost either in Belfast, or, and probably more difficult for me given I had grown up in a city, in the country.

The visits to the countryside, where lanes were unnamed and houses unnumbered, could be and often were a nightmare. To add to my confusion some of the directions given to me were not particularly helpful. There was no satnav then, of course, and at times, after trying to follow the dubious directions provided by my church members, all requiring decades of local knowledge even to begin to put into practice. "You then turn left at Willy's small barn," was not much use when I did not know who Willy was, or how many barns he had, or, indeed, I was left wondering how I could tell if a particular barn was Willy's or not, and having no idea at all about the size of barns, if a barn was large or small.

When the first set of directions proved futile I would scour the countryside for someone to ask directions of. Typically, I always seemed to pick the grey, rainy days when I could drive for miles without finding anyone to ask. At times when I did ask my English accent threw the person off his or her stroke, or brought a surprised or shocked look. Not all were friendly; some were suspicious of this stranger from a far off place. Many tried to be helpful, but often got me lost. On one occasion I remember setting off from home about 11.00am to visit a family, a journey which should have taken about 45 minutes. Almost three hours later I was still trying to find the house. Soon I gave up and went home defeated. That was the day when the advice I was given at the roadside from a very old, bent and dishevelled farmer, was probably the classic of all the responses, "You want Mrs Mac's house, you say. Och,..aye. Easy...Les see naw." Scratching his stubble and removing, replacing and then pushing the filthy cap to the back of his head, he said, "Ye go straight ahead for about 15 minutes and then turn left where the old barn used to be."

It is no wonder that I gave up defeated on this occasion and turned back towards home.

A lot of bull, huge hands and a giggle which would not stop

One visit which stands out amongst so many was the time when we were entertained by a prominent church family. They were so very kind, as were many host families. It was obvious that the house had been given a huge makeover and cleaned up for the occasion. After all it was not every day the potential new minister and his family were coming to tea. Tea, once more, meant that we would sit up at the table in the best room and in a rather awkward and formal atmosphere engage in polite conversation. The husband and wife were ever so kind. They had pulled out all the stops to make it a grand occasion. Freshly scrubbed and dressed in their Sunday church-going clothes. Sharon, the wife, wore a floral print dress. It was obvious that she felt uncomfortable in her unaccustomed attire.

She was a very large lady, built like a man some of the congregation said and stronger than most, not yet out of her twenties. On the family farm just outside the fishing village of White Rock, it was said that Sharon was called on to do all the jobs the men did not want to do. If muscle was needed or there was any hint of danger then the call would go out for Sharon. A kindly, simple soul, Sharon had been the tomboy of the farm, competing with her numerous brothers and male cousins in every way the farm would allow; she had been working with tractors and cows ever since she could walk and probably before she could talk. Once when some stray kittens had found their way deep into the drainage system of the cowshed it was Sharon who took on the task of rescuing them. This entailed digging out a hole going far under the shed and crawling in to reach the strays. The men thought it too risky and not worth the effort.

Sharon was called for if there was a problem with the bull. The herd was walked along the fairly busy main road twice a day, from the field to the milking shed and back again. Twice a day, the large herd held up the traffic for as long as it took while the cows sauntered along on their way to milking, twice a day, every day, even Christmas day. The milk production did not stop for Christmas Day or any other day, for that matter. It was no respecter of public holidays. The whole herd, forty to fifty cows in all, followed by the largest bull I had ever seen, were marched along the public and fairly busy road from field to farm and back again, twice a day. The bull would not stay in the field on his own. He would, I was told, go into a rage, literally a terrible rage, if he was separated from his herd, his harem. The only answer was to walk him in with the cows. And this was fine most of the time as he would follow on behind his girls. But it was made clear to us from many sources; everyone had a story to tell to support the claim, that bulls are very unpredictable animals, indeed.

There were numerous stories told to me on my visits around the farms of farmers who had been trampled to death by the bull they had owned for years, stories of attacks on walkers and the story of the fight to the death between two bulls, one of which had broken out of his own field and ventured into the fields of a neighbouring farm, some three miles away. He was in search of female companionship. The host bull objected to this, as you might imagine, and in the ensuing fight, which lasted most of the night according to local legend, the two, after ripping out a quarter-of-a-mile of barbed wire fencing and fence posts, were still deeply engaged in terrifying combat, until, finally both were shot dead. It was said this was the only way to stop them.

Occasionally, we would hear that Sharon's family bull had misbehaved on the road to the milking shed, at times ending up in a neighbouring garden after crashing through a fence or a hedge. It was always Sharon who took the lead in bringing him to book. Sharon told me that as soon as you got a hold on its nose-ring the bull would be led meekly and mildly, like a lamb. I took her word for it. I also remember seeing a little too much of Sharon on one occasion, when she was in hospital. She had been changing the wheel on the tractor and had an accident. The tractor came off the jack and down upon her leg, breaking it in several places. I visited her in hospital several times as she recovered from the very nasty break. Once she threw off her bedcover to show me the pins which had been inserted in order to keep her broken bones in place until they mended. The long, steel pins protruded from her leg in several places, surrounded by bruises of various colours. A fairly short and uncharacteristic nightie revealed far too much to me of

Sharon's leg and thigh. It was much more than I wanted to see. I hastily averted my eyes.

****

Sharon was a good soul. She was a hard worker both on the farm and in the church. I always felt she got a raw deal in the pecking order in both. One day at Sunday School, for Mother's Day, the children were encouraged to draw a picture and write on it a message for mum to be read out in church as part of the special service. Sharon's six year old daughter drew a picture of her mum, accentuating her size, complete with its message, more than likely picking up and aping words heard at home. Emblazoned along the top of the page was her message for Mother's Day, "My mum is a dirty great brute." Not a typical Mothering Sunday message by any standard. We convinced her that she should not take this picture to display in church, or, indeed, take it home to give to her mum after the service.

Sharon's husband Ben looked equally out of place in his Sunday best when we joined them for tea. He was a thin man, very wiry, who looked much older than his years. The thing which struck us immediately was the size of his hands. His hands were huge, really huge. Without any exaggeration they were the size of dinner plates. I have never seen such large hands before or since. They were honed this way by years and years of hard work in the field.

Sharon and Ben had married late for this culture where teenage marriages were still the norm, although there was the extreme and exceptional case of two of my congregation who had been engaged for 37 years. I understand that about two years after I left Northern Ireland John made an "honest women," as he told people, of his fiancée Betty and they finally married and moved in together as man and wife.

Sharon's parents told us that they were pleased and rather relieved to get her married off. It was a happy marriage and they had been blessed with three children. They were a contented family, who warmly welcomed us to their home that day. However, it was not a relaxing and happy experience for us. We were early into our Northern Irish experience and were not used to the Irish, country and farming ways, all of which combined at times to give us a huge problem of understanding and communication.

In addition, the strong Belfast accent we sometimes encountered made some conversations difficult, to say the least. At times this was made worse by the Ulsterisms, which in the early days confused us no end, but these occasions, difficult though they were, were nothing compared to the visit for tea at Sharon and Ben's during that first summer vacation trip.

Sharon was not a great talker, and when she did her accent was very strong and her vocabulary very limited. Much of her dialogue involved gesticulations, nods, and the word 'aye'. It was difficult enough to sustain a conversation for long on this basis. Poor Ben was worse. He had what we thought might have been a slightly disfigured face on one side; if so, this might have been why he spoke out of the tight corner of one side of his mouth. A hole just enough to hold a cigarette, from memory. And the problem was his thick accent meant that we literally could not understand a word he said. All it was to us was noises. We think that his primary word was the same as his wife's, 'aye', but could not be sure. So it was an extremely difficult afternoon. When Sharon was in the room we got by. We managed to read her body language and gestures and could piece together enough understanding to begin to claim something of a conversation. But when she left the room to prepare the tea, a ham salad I recall (we were strict vegetarians, of course, a fact known to all involved) with breads and cheeses and pickles and many cakes and buns, it became increasingly difficult.

The problem was Ben wanted to converse. He talked away at us both, at times asking questions often pausing for meaningful responses. Our problem was we could not understand him and we felt awful about it. Here were two lovely people making a very big effort to make us more than welcome, and we felt trapped in a most bizarre situation. And there was worse to come.

Now I do not share this in any way to ridicule this couple. Indeed, they were warm and generous to a fault. But it was a difficult and bizarre situation which seemed to go on for ages. And to make matters worse, and this was when I really did get hot under the collar, Angela got the giggles. Anyone who knows my wife will agree there is not a nasty bone in her body. She looks down at no one and is a most compassionate human being. On this occasion, much to her own horror the strain of the situation overtook her; it became too much. Angela got the giggles, and she could not stop. She was not laughing at Ben. It was, I think, a nervous reaction to the situation. And try as she might she could not stop. Just like a naughty student in school when he or she knows that they must not laugh at any cost, but somehow this makes it so much worse. In the end I was kicking Angela's leg under the table and this, too, made it worse. It must have been a nervous reaction. She would not hurt anyone's feelings for the world, but she could not stop. And still Ben talked on at us, occasionally pausing for responses. And still Angela giggled. In fact the more he talked at us and the more we could not understand, the more she giggled. Stuffing her napkin into her mouth she tried to stifle it; biting hard on it, still she giggled. At one point Angela even pretended to drop her napkin on the floor and then not to be able to find it, in order to spend several minutes virtually under the table trying to compose herself; and still she giggled. Then she set me off. Thankfully poor Ben did not even seem to notice and carried on with his one-sided conversation regardless.

I am still not sure as to how we got through the afternoon. We left drained and bemused, with a slightly guilty feeling of having done something wrong. Another stiff drink was called for. Thankfully whenever we saw Ben and Sharon at church or elsewhere after this they were perfectly friendly and there was no hint of any hurt or offence taken. We hoped they thought it was an English eccentricity.

89

Language problems and the "strange Wee-man"

The very first visit we made to Moneymore, a weekend trip when we flew over to meet everyone for the very first time and to discuss the possibility and details of the summer pastorate, provided several examples of the language and communication problems yet to come and should have given us clues as to what we should expect in general in the future. We flew into Belfast, were met by members of the congregation and taken out to the church.

We had been led to believe from telephone conversations that it was a lovely village setting, but nothing could be further from the truth. We arrived at a very grey scene. For a start the sky was very grey, very grey indeed, which did not help. As we drove down the main road into the "village" our hearts sank. It was a fairly depressing picture; one filled with images of grey buildings. Remember the church was grey; the church buildings and manse were grey and all of the executive homes, council houses or social housing to you and me, were grey. A lot had been lost in translation over the telephone. It looked like the grim pictures seen on television of a prison community, or the poor housing I was to experience in Romania two years later, when I flew there from Belfast in an attempt to adopt a child from one of the many orphanages following Ceausescu's fall.

On this first visit we were immediately taken to the church and shown around. There was a welcome committee of some twenty people, all prominent members of the church. Mostly farmers, dressed in their Sunday best, with tight, starched collars and suits which had seen better days. Days when I am sure they had fitted well. They were out in force and after the general introductions they literally followed us around as we were led from the church into the manse. We trailed around every room, shuffling along cramped hallways and in and out of room after room. Everyone apart from us, of course, had been in the manse many, many times over the years, but still they followed on. We led the procession, guided by the Church Secretary, stood for a short while in each vacant room – the previous minister had moved out with his belongings into retirement a few years before – and moved on to the next, all whilst being followed around by the human chain of important church people. And the most bizarre thing of all was the silence. Apart from the Secretary announcing that this was bedroom number "One," then "Two," "Three," "Four," and "Five," and this was the kitchen, lounge or study as we slowly made our way around this large double fronted house, we stood in each room in an uncomfortable and tangible silence.

Even stranger was the invite to see the "hot press." We had no idea what this was. It turned out to be the airing cupboard. We gazed into it, again in silence, and moved on. It was like some bizarre ritual. The Ideal Home Exhibition turned on its head. There we used to queue and follow a line to see things on display. Now there was nothing to see

91

and people were sort of queuing and following a line to see us.

Trying to make polite conversation was ever so difficult. Often we could not make sense of the Ulsterisms, this compounded by the heavy accent made dialogue at best nearly impossible. Sometimes confusion abounded, like over the 'hot press.' There were many examples of this.

****

Over the months we encountered many strange discrepancies in translation, but we soon got the hang of them. We soon discovered that "bun" meant cake or pastry, an "executive home" was not an expensive maisonette or middle class, five bedroom, detached home, but a small, grey, two-up-two-down council house, and that the *Telegraph*, which often was quoted at me as if was an infallible oracle of truth and prediction by the farmers, the elderly on the council estate and by the least likely Telegraph readers you could imagine, or at least I thought so, was not actually the broadsheet we knew from home, but the *Belfast Telegraph*, which was a sort of a local paper, as well as covering major national and international issues in its early pages. There were other local papers, of course, the *Newtonards Chronicle* and so on, and church events would be advertised in all of these and follow up reports and pictures would soon appear; but there was nothing like the *Telegraph* for most of my congregation, the *Belfast Telegraph,* that was.

It was in the *Telegraph* that most of the deaths of members of my congregation were announced, with details of the funerals and what to do with flowers or donations. The instructions often requested that donations, perhaps for the hospice or hospital or Action Cancer, should be sent to me, the minister to collect up and send on to the charity of choice. Rev Kilty, he who warned us on the very dark and not slightly scary first night of our arrival that the IRA would know that we were there, regularly told us and anyone else who would listen that he would check the *Telegraph* each evening, there were two editions each day, one early and one late, to see if his name appeared in the obituary column. He said if it did not he would breathe a sigh of relief and know that he was ok; God had spared him for at least another day.

****

We were at first puzzled to say the least when we heard a number of the sweet old ladies of the congregation refer to our youngest Andy as being "strange." Perhaps not the best way to describe someone's "Wee-man," as they also affectionately called him as the months passed and he grew into a toddler. 'Wee-man' sounded quite sweet, but 'strange;' this left us more than a bit bemused. It was usually after a service or church meeting, perhaps during the "Teas" (another Ulsterism), the ladies wanted to take him away from mum or big sister Alex, to hold, pet and fuss him. Generally, he would kick up a real fuss, and he did have a terrific pair of lungs on him as he more than ably demonstrated publicly on the fateful evening of his baptism some weeks ahead.

We began to wonder, was there something wrong with him which we and the doctors at the Royal had failed to spot, but was now being picked up and exposed by the old, wily country born and bred matriarchs of the congregation, who were experienced in these things and had seen it all before? Were they seeing signs of something we could not, just like some of the farmers swore they could predict the weather far more accurately than that "Fish man on BBC" by observing the behaviour of their livestock and the buds and things on the trees. Many times I was told that we were in for a wet spell or a windy spell or that the red holly berries meant this or that for the coming days and they would have to get the cows out for a bit (from the cow shed?), or put them back in. All of this was quite beyond us, of course, with our East End background. If we wanted to have even the slightest idea what the weather would be like, we did what we thought most people did, we watched the weather forecast on TV or simply looked out of the window.

After a few weeks unable to contain our natural intrigue and because of the distinctly uncomfortable feeling we had each time someone said, "Och, bless him, he is wee bit strange," we finally plucked up the courage to ask. Aware we could so easily offend people in this the early stages of my ministry – we had heard many tales from experienced colleagues as to what congregations could be like and how difficult a minister's life could be if he upset some of the congregation who were after all his employer and paymaster – we made our enquiries of one of the sweet old ladies who often used the term when she was alone with us in the manse.

I twittered rather. "Sorry, Mrs Williams, what does 'a bit strange' actually mean? We...er... I...um... have no idea what people mean by this here. I, um...we..in England it means something is wrong with someone,.. um .....you know... that someone is a bit odd."

Mrs Williams was truly shocked: how could we have even imagined that anyone would think that the lovely Wee-man had something wrong with him, or that he was odd. How could we even imagine such a thing? She then explained to us that all 'strange' meant was that he was a bit shy, no more and no less.

****

So, many of our early conversations were complicated to say the least. We soon got used to these differences and even adopted some; for example Andy became known to us also as the Wee-man, a cute and lovely description, we thought, of a small boy. Although I think he was to become fed up with the numerous times he was told how much the Wee-man looked like his daddy. It was strange to us how many people in their fifties and sixties, with children, and in some cases grandchildren, of their own still referred to their own parents, both living and dead, as "Mammy and Pappy." This seemed a little strange to us.

A very harsh accent indeed

The Northern Irish accent to our hearing was very harsh. The girls being of school age and mixing with children all day (only Protestant children, of course, as the education system provided mostly separate and segregated schools for Protestant children and Roman Catholic children) soon picked up the local accent, Alex particularly so. She took to it immediately, and she must have had a natural capacity for it or a greater need to fit in, being that bit older than Faith, because within hours of our arrival, or so it seemed to us, she was talking away with a very strong Belfast accent. We used to tease her that she sounded more Irish then the Irish at times. Truthfully, at first, we were not quite sure about this. We were certainly not snobs, and we would never look down on anyone for any sort of regional accent, but whilst we understood the need for the children to blend in and not stick out like sore thumbs by speaking differently, we were not sure about it; it was not something we had even thought about.

It must have been hard enough for the children being the children of the manse and having every move scrutinized and commented upon by all and sundry. I well remember the uproar it caused when Alex took a ruler from another pupil at school. It was a silly prank sort of a thing, nothing malicious, or too serious, but Alex was a child of the manse, the minister's daughter, as she was reminded more than once in the commotion which followed as we were called into school to see the teacher. So we appreciated the need for the children to fit in, or to stand out as little as possible, given they had not been born into this tight-knit community, where everyone was connected or related if you went back far enough in the records or in the memories of the country folk. We appreciated their need to speak like everyone else.

Faith was starting school for the first time at the local primary school. The school had grown out of the original village school, which had been started by the church for the village children. It had long ago been moved by the council along the road and developed on a site just beyond the church grounds. The church no longer had any responsibility for it, long since relinquishing it to the local authority. The old church-school building still existed, yet another grey stone building owned by the church, and was called the Old School. It was used for the odd church meeting and a playgroup met there on a weekly basis. I became a governor of the village primary school by virtue of my office as local minister. I would often pop in to take assemblies, or the odd RE lesson, and would always attend the school Nativity play, and try to get to the Christmas Panto, at which the head master, a lovely, lively and popular man, displayed a tendency to dress up as a dame of some description or other, always a dame.

****

Angela attended the playgroup at the Old School with Andy. I remember visiting regularly and chatting to the mums and the toddlers, as yet another function of my ministry. One Christmas they were holding a short carol service and party but were short of a Santa. I was press ganged into service and dressed up in the overlarge red suit, stuffed out with many pillows. All belted up, I donned the beard and made my way down the street to the Old School.

We have a wonderful Polaroid photograph of our Weeman sitting on my lap. He was about two and a half and he did not see beyond the fake beard to recognize it was really me his pappy (actually, we did not go as far as adopting this term). Later on that day in the manse, he tried to go into great detail about how they had received a visit from Santa. He sat there on the sofa, with eyes still wide, telling me all about it. Little did he know.

****

Yes, to us, the Northern Irish accent, at its worst, was an extremely harsh one. It was, at least to our hearing as far as the Protestant community were concerned, very similar to the harshest of Scottish accents. After all, these parts, the north-eastern region of Ireland, had been populated largely by the settlers from Scotland in the great Plantation of Ulster from 1606, which involved displacing the native Irish from their lands and installing the settlers and landowners who commanded the political and economic power.

Many of my congregation and the wider Protestant community could trace their family's history back to the Plantation, and some still considered themselves to be defenders of the land acquired then. There were still strong links to Scotland. It was only a few miles across the Irish Sea at the narrowest point and on a clear day the Mull of Kintyre could be clearly seen from points on the Antrim Coast.

Many of the Protestant people I met were supporters of Glasgow Rangers Football Club, whereas the other side of the sectarian divide favoured Celtic. Even football was infected by sectarianism. Some will recall the unfortunate incident in 1998 when Paul Gascoigne jigged and danced around as he mimed playing an imaginary flute in front of the Celtic supporters, mimicking the flutes played by many at the Protestant Orange Lodge parades on the 12th of July. For Gascoigne this may have been an act of clowning about, but for many it was inflammatory behaviour, with heavy sectarian overtones.

This event was witnessed by millions of live TV viewers and England manager, Glenn Hoddle, who was in the stands. The last time Gascoigne did this, in a pre-season tournament, he later admitted on TV that a motorist queuing next to him at traffic lights threatened to slit his throat if he did it again. This time he was fined £20,000 by Rangers and was subjected to IRA death threats for several months after the incident.

At best, if done flippantly, it was an insensitive and silly act. At worst, if done with full awareness it could be seen as inflammatory and unforgivable, especially given the thousands of lives which have been lost or destroyed and the suffering caused by the land and political claims of the two factions.

Even as I am putting my memories down on paper for this book, there are reports of a display of anti-British sentiment at a Celtic football match near to Remembrance Day 2010. One headline and report of the protest read:

THERE is outrage after scores of Celtic football fans held banners describing the remembrance poppy as "bloodstained"

The protest staged by a section of the Glasgow club's fans saw six large banners held up ahead of a game on Saturday in opposition to the team wearing poppies on their shirts next weekend. The banners, organised by an extreme group of Celtic fans, included one which said"no bloodstained poppies on our hoops." Another carried the slogan "Your deeds would shame all the devils in Hell" above the words "Ireland, Iraq, Afghanistan."

These things never seem to disappear completely. They seem to be never far under the surface.

****

There most certainly is a long historical connection between Northern Ireland and Scotland. Even today, I am told, Scottish lodges journey across the Irish Sea to offer their support at the annual Protestant Orange parades on the 12th of July. A strong connection to Scotland through historical roots, people's names, names which were said to give away on which side of the divide someone belonged, not from choice but by birth, even the choice of football team; and to our untrained ears, at times, the accent. It was at its worst a very harsh one.

"Boys-oh-boy," (to use an Ulsterism) the accent in places was harsh. At worst even a "good morning" could sound like a threat.

Thankfully, the girls did not adopt the harshest accent, but a rather gentle and pleasant lilt. We did receive the occasional, "What about ye," from them, but we accepted this and the lilt as a positive part of their acclimatisation. After all, our plan, if you can plan so far ahead, was to stay in Northern Ireland for many, many years. It was something of an irony that we knew of a number of, how shall I say it, the more professional families who were sending their children to weekly elocution lessons to complete or soften their vowels, indeed to try to install in their Northern Irish off-spring more of an educated English accent, perhaps what we would have at one time called a BBC accent.

It was, it seemed, rather ironic that people were paying very good money and putting in a lot of time and effort for their children to adopt a good English accent when we were coming in from the opposite direction, so to speak. Our children were acquiring, quite naturally, and without the cost of weekly lessons, a soft, thankfully, Belfast brogue. However, on reflection we were not too bothered; we both had grown up with and grown out of a fairly harsh cockney accent. I had deliberately schooled myself away from this not out of some kind of snobbery, but I had soon realized when I started preaching that my accent rather grated on some, when something was 'sumfink', and nothing was 'nuffink', especially when I travelled my way around the home counties. I wanted people to concentrate more on what I was saying as I delivered my sermons and prayers each week at a different place of worship, rather than focusing on my accent. I did not want my lead in to silent prayer to sound like a scene from East Enders.

So, no longer did I speak like a Cockney, but I am sure that it was and still is quite obvious that Angela and I came from the London area, or the south-east. We had not "gone posh," as my father would have said, even if I had broken the mould and did what was not the norm for our sort of people, the working class, and got myself an education, this after spectacularly failing to achieve at school. I had gone to one of the worst comprehensive schools in the East End of London, leaving at sixteen, labelled 'thick', with the bare minimum of qualifications: three or four very poor grade CSE's. I was not allowed to take the O-levels in those subjects, except the English one, which I failed.

So, Angela and I had no problems with the pleasant Irish lilt which the girls now had, and we assumed that the Wee-man would grow up with it, too. We considered that we were in for the long haul. We had not uprooted ourselves from family and friends, few of whom would brave the dangers they had seen on TV to come and visit us. Actually in the five years we were there none of our family ever came over, and only a few friends, four couples, one leaving their children behind, and a single friend. We often thought perhaps we would retire there, after serving several generations of my congregation, over several decades. This was not the way it turned out.

****

The church I was in and the wider denomination had a tradition of long, long, ministries. With some ministers staying in the same post for decades, literally decades: thirty, forty, fifty or even more years. One colleague retired whilst I was there who had been the minister of the same church for more than sixty years. As I was frequently told, ministers are not allowed to retire, they die in harness.

Many, if not most, of the ministers I knew, and knew of, worked on way beyond retirement age. I guess the routine was so ingrained into them there was no possibility of stopping out of choice. The "calling" which brought them into this was a total way of life: a life which was all consuming, hugely demanding and offered little financial reward. Perhaps some of these ministers were not in a position financially to retire, having lived on a fairly paltry Stipend and in a house which went with the job. What else was there for it but to work on? Mind you no one came into ministry for the financial rewards. This was just as well considering I was told by a senior minister the congregation's favourite prayer was, "Lord you keep our minister humble and we will keep him poor." I am sure this was said to me with tongue-in-cheek, but it had more than a grain of truth to it.

Most of the ministers I knew were more than well educated and would have had no problem entering any of the usual lucrative professions open to graduates in those days. I had spent six years in full-time training, five reading theology, one more to complete a teaching qualification, and then several years part-time studying Philosophy. The teaching qualification was taken as a sort of insurance policy on the kindly advice of a very wise elderly minister, whom I met at Oxford. He had been around the tracks rather and had lots of experience of congregations and how a minister could be treated. For a start he tried to put me off from even entering training for the ministry. This was after I had successfully completed the very stringent interviews, including an assessment of my psychological suitability. His advice not to go ahead with my plans to train was for my own good and not because I was unsuitable. At least I think that was the case! But my sense of calling was too strong. I ignored his initial advice.

However, I am ever thankful I did follow his second piece of advice and undertook the extra year to complete a teaching qualification. It has served us wonderfully well over the years, at times making the difference between financial survival or not, with the pay from my two or three days a week supply teaching, where and when I could get it, providing money for groceries, literally putting the food on the table for my young family. This was especially vital after I left my first congregation following an unfortunate fall out with several key and powerful families there who effectively ran the church. It was a time when we were very poor, really very poor. At this time it was said of us by a brother minister and colleague, "We will starve them out."

A soldier crouching by a wall, a chilling advert and "First hang all the priests and then set them on fire as just hanging is too good for them," he said

As the time went on we experienced more and more of the sinister underbelly of the Province. On the surface life appeared pretty normal. People went about their daily lives, and most were preoccupied with family life, shopping and paying the bills and planning the summer holiday. We may have been scared witless on that first night, concerned that the IRA knew we were there and further alarmed by the experience of Bill and Margaret's innocent drive in the Mourne Mountains, but bombs and bullets were not on every street corner. We got on with our lives, and I worked around the clock to establish myself in my ministry.

This is not what our family and friends thought, of course. For a start they all thought we were mad to choose Northern Ireland over some quiet congregation in a leafy southern English town or village. I have already said our family would not come over to see us or the new baby. Few friends would take the risk, either. We were very much left to our own devices. The image in the popular mind, including the minds of our family and friends, was of bombs and bullets on every street corner. This was not the case. Much of life went on as normal. The regular acts of terrorism seemed to be absorbed into and accommodated within ordinary life, even accepted it seemed. Indeed, it was as if it had become part of normality for the many of the people of Northern Ireland.

The people were remarkably resilient. Life went on: parties, picnics and pantomimes. It was just that there was a strong underlying current. The Troubles were never far away. Almost every news item told of another shooting, murder or bombing, or of bungled attempts, or knee-capping, the favoured form of punishment of the paramilitaries. Unless it was a major event on a large scale, a particularly vicious atrocity, it hardly seemed to raise an eyebrow. The people had seen it all before. They simply got on with life.

Life was affected, of course. Some of my congregation would not travel into Belfast or parts of it, others would not feel comfortable there; some would not go to the seaside town of Newcastle as it was close to the border, or to the Mournes for the same reason. The regular police and Army roadblocks, the visible Army presence, when they were on street patrols, the body and bag searches which we had to undergo to get into a store in Belfast, all had an impact on life. The disruption to travel caused by a coded warning call to the newspapers or radio station to say a bomb had been planted in a specific location, real or hoax warnings, caused chaos. Roads were blocked, shops and houses cleared, areas sealed off until the bomb squad did its stuff and pronounced the area safe, perhaps after a controlled explosion of a badly positioned but completely innocent vehicle parked nearby. We were often warned by the congregation, "Do not park anywhere illegally, badly, in an odd place or position, especially in the centre of Belfast or near to a police station anywhere, else you are likely to come back with your shopping and find you no longer have a car in one piece."

A favoured method of the terrorists, we were told, was to hijack at gunpoint several cars and lorries, park them up in different parts of the city and then ring with a warning to say they had been packed with explosives. Some had been. Others were decoys. The idea was to cause as much disruption and fear as possible. You can imagine the chaos and gridlock which ensued, tying up the security forces and the city for hours. One member of my congregation, a man in his 50s who delivered bread for his living, was hijacked and blindfolded at gunpoint for this purpose. He and his lorry were taken to a house in West Belfast, somewhere off the Falls Road, he thought, and he was to have a terrifying experience, which affected him for many years. He was told his lorry had been packed with explosives and that he had to drive it to an Army checkpoint and tell them what was on board. They also told him his own address and all the names of his family and that he must do as he was told. He did. He subsequently had to retire from work early on health grounds. He experienced the effects of long term stress and panic attacks, and he went into a terrible panic when driving in the city if car pulled alongside his vehicle.

The Troubles were never far away.

****

It seemed to us that most people had grown accustomed to it all and perhaps in some way had become de-sensitized to what was happening all around them. We were not. After all, these people had lived through this for more than twenty-five years. A whole generation had known nothing else. It had become a way of life, and at the time there seemed to be no end in sight. Many young people it seemed to us used education to get away from it, a way to escape from the pressures of living on top of this time-bomb. One member of the congregation had four grown-up children all of whom had chosen to go to university in England and had decided to stay and set up life there when they graduated. It seemed to us there was a possible brain drain in this respect. To compound it we were told of a diminishing Protestant population and an ever increasing Roman Catholic one. No wonder tensions were high. A big population change could result in a big political change through the democratic process.

But we were not born and bred there. We had not grown up with these tragic events colouring our lives. We were very sensitive to it all, very sensitive indeed; most certainly in the early times. Angela will never forget the first time she encountered a full and armed-to-the-hilt British Army foot patrol. I was visiting in Lisburn, about ten miles from Belfast, to the south-west and on the River Lagan, in Co Antrim.

110

Angela and the children had come along for the ride and to get to know a little more of another part of the Province, where two or three of our church members lived. I had dropped Angela and the children near some shops with the children so she could buy them some sweets and have a look around. They were doing just this when they suddenly turned a corner and came face to face with a soldier crouching at the side of a wall by a shop, his automatic weapon at the ready. He was surveying the scene before him through its sight. He was part of a patrol. Lisburn had a reputation for sectarian trouble, as did almost many, many places in the Province.

Later, in the car coming home, Angela said that she had felt herself go weak at the knees with fear as she came face-to-face with the wrong end of the automatic rifle. She hurried the children past and was sort of caught up with the rest of the patrol. These very young Englishmen, she said they were boys really, were walking, zigzagging, back and forth across the road and so on, in what was obviously a well practised routine. The "out-runners" suddenly crouching behind a hedge, car or wall, anything it seems to offer them some shelter and protection from a possible attack. They in turn offered cover and protection against an attack on their patrol. When the patrol had caught up another runner or two would go ahead. And so they passed by. It was quite chilling for Angela and Alex, who was old enough to understand, but Faith was too young to take it on, and she was far more interested in her sweeties.

Interestingly and somewhat of a concern to us was that over the months we began to recognize that we become less and less sensitive to what was happening, we were becoming de-sensitized to what we were seeing and hearing. It became just another road block or Army patrol, and we would think nothing more of it.

This was also true of the chilling advert which regularly used to cut into the normal television adverts. We would be watching a programme and then the intermission brought the standard fare: adverts for soap, shampoo, baked beans or bread, and so on. However, the next one started with the chilling image of a masked gunman knocking at a front door and when the door was opened by an unsuspecting child or the lady of the house, he would burst in. On finding his target, the man of the house, the gunman would open fire. The voiceover would then caution us to do all we could to stop the terrorists and to call the 0800 free-phone help-line to report even the merest of whispers of information to the security forces. We were told that even the smallest detail might save lives.

The first time we saw this in the comfort of our own front room, sitting there with the children cosy in front of the fire, we were very shocked. But, after just a few weeks, we thought almost nothing of it. It was different when the Troubles came much closer to home.

****

Most people we got to know through the church and beyond had lost a loved one or had someone close to them terribly injured, or knew of someone who had been affected by the violence of the past 25 years. Our neighbour Ray's mum had lost both her legs in an explosion; his cousin Bill had been shot; Sue's uncle had been murdered. We met a number of police officers who had lost colleagues and now lived under intense stress having to take exceptional precautions to protect themselves against the very real fear of reprisals for being a member of the security forces. It seems that they were seen as a legitimate target, even off duty or retired. We knew a family who lived near to us; both husband and wife were police officers. Each time they used their cars they would search under them with a mirror on a pole to make sure no explosive device had been placed underneath. They told us they regularly took a different route home from work and used a car pool with ever changing number plates, all to throw off the scent anyone trying to gather intelligence information about them and to minimize the chances of an attack. It was said that bullet-proof glass had been installed at their home. They told us they always carried their handguns, even when off duty; and they were very careful not go into certain areas, even for a day out with the children at the coastal town of Newcastle, because of the possible danger.

****

I remember being extremely shocked during a visit to a small home on the village estate, one of the executive homes, when a young man of about eighteen or nineteen years of age looked me straight in the face and said in all sincerity that all priests should be "hanged and then set alight, as just hanging was too good for them." His mother, perhaps more than a little embarrassed by his outburst during my visit of all things, tried to suggest he didn't really mean it, to which he replied, "I f***ing well did," and then repeated it in case anyone had the slightest doubt about his feelings, "We should hang and burn the lot of them, the priests and all the Taigs." "If we don't," he added, as if it were some kind of justifying rationale, "they will drive us into the sea."

A siege mentality and an eerie silence on the Shankill Road

At times a siege mentality was very apparent. Some people were especially suspicious of strangers. I remember being with another minister and taking some furniture up and over the border into Donegal. He was doing a favour for a friend who had a holiday home there and had hired a van and enlisted my help for the day. It was a long drive to the far costal region. After dropping off the furniture, an hour or so into the return journey we decided to stop at a pub for a pint and some food. As we walked into the fairly crowded bar everyone stopped talking and turned to stare straight at us. The presence of strangers, especially two English strangers, was noted and brought a strange hush about the place. We pressed on and ordered a pint of Guinness and a meal each, but it was not a comfortable time.

I had a worse experience much closer to home during the first summer experience, just around the corner to the manse. I had just set out to visit the members of the congregation who lived closest to the manse, those with a proper addresses, streets with proper names and houses with numbers on them, unlike the many visits made deep into the country where more often than not I got lost, often through following the very dubious directions provided by someone in my congregation, or by a local who just happened to chance by.

On this occasion, close to the manse, very enthusiastic and keen, all ready to get going and meet my congregation in their own homes, I walked along the main street through the village, eyeing the numbers and looking at the papers in my hand on which was written my probably overly ambitious and extensive visiting rota for the day, all drawn up by me very early that morning over breakfast.

As I pondered the house before me a rusty car pulled up at the kerbside. It was a pretty battered heap, as were the three men sitting inside. They did look a real motley crew, unshaven, covered in tattoos and with a very aggressive look about them, a look matched by their attitudes.

"Who the f*** are you and what are you f***ing doing here," aggressively demanded the one in the front passenger seat, furiously winding down the window. As I was about to reply, a pit bull terrier, I think it was a pit bull, either that or something very similar, threw itself at the rear side-window with such force I thought it would crash straight through it.

I think my accent threw them a bit as I had to repeat what I said a couple of times as they continued to question and press me about my business there. It was obvious that they had spotted my presence on the village estate. I was a stranger and stood out like a sore thumb.

They must have accepted my story that I was the student pastor at Moneymore Church and was there for an eight-week stint that summer. Without a further word they drove off, leaving me with a slightly uncomfortable feeling.

116

So the Troubles were never too far away. Even the most reasonable and nicest of people, not all of course, but many, would suddenly surprise us with a prejudiced comment. It seemed that if we scratched deep enough most people would reveal a side that hitherto had been hidden. We would see this later when one of the nicest and most generous souls you could wish to meet revealed another side to us on the day she called by unexpectedly to the manse. On that day we had a family visiting. No problem with that, you might think, except that the family happened to be Roman Catholic.

****

One of the ladies in my congregation once said to me, "When the chips are down you are on this side of it or the other, Reverend Rowley, that is just the way it is." She added for good measure and to make sure that I had understood what she was trying to explain to me, and I stress that she was deadly serious as she leant towards me with a poker face and said, "In this place you either kick with your left leg or you kick with your right leg, and that is that. And there is nothing in between, so there's not. Nothing in between."

Biting hard on my lip, I tried desperately hard not to laugh. I could not believe what she had just said. I am

117

convinced to this day she had no idea of what she had just said and how funny it sounded, or perhaps it was just me and my mind, and my way of dealing with the stresses of ministry in Northern Ireland? However the events which often burst into normal life were far from being funny.

The awful tit-for-tat killings which so often dominated the news, especially prevalent during the last eighteen months of our time in Northern Ireland, brought terror to all sections of the community and were impossible to ignore as they broke right into and through the normal life most people were trying to establish. The escalating spiral of violence was especially visible to us during the last months or so of our time in the Province. It was it seemed to us all to de-rail the increasing moves towards peace and a power sharing. Huge strides have been made over the ensuing twenty-years or so, even if we still hear of the occasional acts of terrorism, but by and large it is nothing like the period leading up to the peace established in 1994.

Then horrific events dominated. And it was getting worse. On the 23rd of October, 1993 a terrible atrocity took place on the Shankill Road. The Shankill Road, the name comes from the Irish Seanchill, meaning old church, is the arterial road leading through what is known to be a very rough, tough, working class area of Belfast. The Shankill is a loyalist area, some of it marked out by the red, white and blue of the Union Flag and the red, white and blue of the painted kerb stones. You could never be in doubt about this being a unionist, or loyalist, area. You had only to look at the many wall murals, the wonderfully colourful and always very professional wall paintings which adorned the side of many shops and houses, marking out a territory and spelling out a message. I am thinking here of the graphic pictures on the walls at Freedom Corner as it was called at the top end of Newtownards Road in Belfast; wonderful art work, but a chilling message.

Many of these paintings contained both the gunman, complete with machine gun, and the Bible. The bullet and the Bible, with the Bible open, making a theological statement, I was told, about the Protestant tradition of encouraging the people to go directly to the Word of God, with no need for the Roman Catholic's priestly class to mediate and translate God's teaching of forgiveness. Religion and politics were seen to go hand-in-hand: a heady mix. If you were a Protestant you were seen to be a loyalist, and if you were a Roman Catholic you were seen to be a Republican, despite many Protestants and Roman Catholics perhaps having no strong political views. You either kicked with your left foot or your right foot (the usual version of the saying), and that was it, and there was nothing "in between," as I was told by the lady who confused legs and feet and left me stifling a giggle. But, if at times laughter was a way of dealing with things, the events themselves were deadly serious and never too far away.

****

On the 23rd of October, 1993, two bombers went into Frizzell's fish and chip shop where people were queuing to get their lunch. The IRA claimed that there was to be a meeting of the leaders of the loyalist paramilitaries, the UFF (Ulster Freedom Fighters) and the UDA (Ulster Defence Association). This was the target for the bomb. It happened to be above a fish and chip shop on the Protestant Shankill Road.

The time-bomb went off as it was being planted. Nine people were killed, including two children, in addition to one of the two bombers, Thomas Begley. The building collapsed.

This act resulted in a spate of revenge attacks by the loyalists. In the next few weeks nineteen people were killed by the UVF (Ulster Volunteer Force) or the UDA .These were mostly random revenge killings. For example, eight people died when three UFF members entered the Rising Sun bar in Greysteel, County Londonderry. At the time a Halloween party was going on. It is rumoured that as the three produced an Ak-47 and an automatic pistol and opened fire into the packed crowd, one was said to have called out "Trick or treat."

The victims just happened to be in a certain area, a Roman Catholic area, and were targeted randomly for this and this alone. It was that random, totally unpredictable and that made it all the more chilling.

The day after the bombing of the fish and chip shop on the Shankill Road, I was driving through the area on route to a meeting for reconciliation taking place in the north of Belfast. There was an eerie silence and what I can only describe as a palpable fear in the air as I made my way slowly up the Shankill Road. Part of the road was cordoned off by the police and Army, the security presence was immense, especially near to the former site of the fish and chip shop which had been blown apart. The most chilling thing was the crowds of people. Always after these large scale events the people gathered, some around churches, some close to the scene, faces etched with fear, shock or anger.

People of both sides of the sectarian divide then waited for it to happen, the reprisal, for sooner or later it would come. They all knew it would come.

Weddings, a ride in a helicopter and "blown out of bed," or so she said and still claims

Our daughter Alex still talks about the time she was blown out of bed. Well, she does if any one reminds her of the occasion. The experience is as real to her now as when it happened. At the time we were not quite convinced that it did happen, but she maintains to this day some twenty years or more later that this is exactly what happened. That she was blown out of bed by a bomb blast. It had started off as such an ordinary evening, as well.

I had left the family in the manse doing everything that a normal family would be doing on a dark evening: watching TV, playing games, doing homework and so on; then a bath and off to bed for a read, and then lights off and to sleep. I had left them to go into the church to take a young couple through a wedding rehearsal. This was normal practice. It turned out to be a very far from normal, indeed.

I officiated at many weddings during my time in Northern Ireland and they were all, without exception, hugely enjoyable, if demanding and time consuming. Marriage was, and probably still is, a firm part of the God ordered scheme of things for the people there. It was still a very conservative culture. Most young people followed the

122

traditional pattern of a short engagement and then got on with approaching the minister of the family church about the wedding. This was, of course, to be held in the church where generations of family members had been "hatched, matched or despatched." The church to which the annual Stipend fee was paid religiously to preserve burial rights, the right to be buried in the family grave, and to guarantee the services of the minister at times of need and for the occasional services to mark the rites of passage. Thus it was that many young couples found their way to the manse to be interviewed to ensure that I was happy that their intentions were honourable. Back then, and possibly still now, the minister issued the official paperwork to allow the couple to marry, unlike here in England where much of the official paperwork was carried out at the Registrar's Office by the Registrar.

The minister was also expected to attend the reception following the wedding service, usually restricted to the family and closest of friends, often to act as Master of Ceremonies. Singing for my supper, I often felt. Given that the reception could be a fair distance away from the church, and all of the waiting around for the photographs and speeches and so on, which we all recognize as a normal part of the wedding scene, it all took an awful lot time out of a very busy schedule. I once raised the issue with key members of my congregation. I put it to them that I was happy to attend a reception where possible, but given I had a young family which I rarely saw I might politely decline an invitation at some point. There was a powerful silence and then a "tut-tut-tutting." Followed by, "You have to go," and

"The ministers have always gone." Finally, from another, "People won't like it if you don't." I was soon put in my place. And so off I went. Following the wedding service, which occurred most of the time on a Saturday (sometimes there were two on a Saturday); it was off to the reception. Then, on Sunday, it was back to the usual round of services, usually one, but sometimes two or even three, depending on the time of year or the needs of local churches which were "vacant" (without minister).

Back in the manse, after a stringent, but friendly interview, talking through what they would like on their wedding day, and after lots of form filling in and proving of identities, the couple would be invited to attend church for a number of Sundays over the months leading up to the big day, unless, of course, they were already regular attendees. Then it was the final run-in to the big day. All the preparations were in place, the hotel reception and honeymoon all booked for many months and everyone expectant. The rehearsal at the church came next. A run through to make sure everyone knew their battle stations, as I called them, for the big day.

The rehearsal would take at least an hour, sometimes more than two. The couple, their parents, siblings and all the key players for the day would be there, including all the ushers, page boys and bridesmaids, and so on. Often other family members, aunts and uncles, grandparents and more, would turn up as well, all turning out to see the show, wishing not to miss the slightest bit of the occasion. The florist, the church caretaker and the organist would also be

124

there, and just about anyone else who happened to be passing who wanted a free show. We would then rehearse, and I mean rehearse in every single detail, each and every aspect of the service, including practising the vows and responses, omitting the names of the couple, of course, in case there was any doubt that they had actually been married by mistake on the dry run. Such it was on the night when Alex claimed she had been blown out of bed by the blast of a bomb.

****

Most of the weddings I conducted in Northern Ireland were larger than life affairs. Families must have planned and saved for many months, if not years, in order to fulfil the traditional obligations. All credit to them. In some cases it was said, it was a matter of outdoing a previous wedding of a neighbour's child, or even a wedding within their own family. Perhaps outdoing is too strong a term to use and it was more a case of not letting the side down. I recall the lavish wedding of one member of the congregation and the beautiful pony and antique open-top carriage hired for the day to ferry the bride to the church and the bride and groom to the hotel after the service. It was beautiful, highly polished and gleaming, as was the pony. The problem was the Northern Irish weather. It did not need Michael Fish to tell us that rain was likely. Rain was always likely in Northern Ireland, an ever present threat. And rain it did. Apparently, just as the poor bride left the comfort of her parents' home the dark-grey sky finally gave up its burden and the heavens opened. An incessant stream of stair-rods bombarded the open-top carriage throughout the journey to the church. It wasn't a long journey, but long enough. The poor bride was absolutely drenched. Make-up and hair ruined, dress sodden and bridesmaids bedraggled beyond recognition, they stoically carried on. They will never forget their special day. It was such a terrible shame for them.

Other weddings come to mind, for example, the wedding of a member of the security forces. In Northern Ireland this was a term applied to either Army personnel or policemen, or policewomen (this is how they were known then, with little regard for the political correctness which has dominated life in more recent years), or in some eyes an ex-member of either. Whether still serving, or having served in either many years ago, it was enough to make the person a target in the eyes of the paramilitaries. Indeed, a few days before our return to England in 1994 we were caught up in a small queue of cars in a tiny village on the outskirts of Belfast, moments after a shooting had occurred and the police had just arrived to block the road. The man who was murdered had been a member of the forces some twenty-five years before, and now, many years later, as he was going innocently about his business as a butcher, a gunman walked into his shop and shot him dead, just a few minutes before we passed by.

Given this situation it was no wonder that any place where off duty or ex-police or Army personnel gathered was seen as a special risk. A wedding was no exception. For this reason, the evening before these weddings the church grounds and buildings were searched and an armed guard posted to ensure that that they would not be tampered with overnight. Then on the day of the wedding more searches, a visible armed presence around the church and at times armed plainclothes officers amidst the congregation. Thankfully for me such experiences were few and far between. Weddings were high enough pressure at the best of times, with the often very nervous bride and groom liable to faint, giggle nervously and uncontrollably or fluff their lines.

My job was to steer the couple through it all, making sure all the legalities were completed without error. My senior colleagues stressed that even the smallest of spelling mistakes on the documentation could nullify the marriage. Moreover, I had to give them a good show and make sure they were married in style. I often heard my wedding services compared to those of local ministers by visiting members of the family and friends. I never took too much notice when I heard any comparisons, positive or negative.

Of course, the emotion of the occasion often took over from the reality. I remember being present to assist Rev Kilty, the elderly and very experienced minister who had warned us of the IRA knowing we were there in the Province, and standing bemused as he droned on and on, giving the most incomprehensible and garbled address about the merits of marriage and keeping a home. I think this was his theme although it was very unclear and at several points he mentioned his own ducks and geese. After the service, with me preparing to defend an elderly colleague against many critical comments from angry relatives, the grandfather of the bride, moved to tears by the occasion, waxed lyrical about the Rev Kilty and his wonderful address.

****

The wedding which stands out the most for me for selfish reasons was a very grand affair indeed. It was the wedding of a young relative of a very wealthy man who owned a string of carpet and curtain shops across the whole of Ireland. The reception was to take place in what was and still is considered to be one of the best hotels in Northern Ireland, or indeed the whole of Ireland, the Slieve Donard Hotel, set amidst the Mourne Mountains and close to the sea. It was very, very high class, a very posh do. The hotel, set in six acres, "nestling" at the foot of the Mournes, still boasts of its luxurious surroundings and having one of the world's top golf courses, the Royal County Down.

The wedding reception, to which I, as custom dictated, was duly invited, was very elaborate, and it must have cost an absolute fortune. The crowning glory and the best bit by miles, as far as I was concerned, was the entertainment laid on during the burden of the photographs to save guests becoming too bored whilst waiting, a helicopter, offering trips around the bay at Newcastle and over the mountains. I recall thinking, "How the other half live."

I had never been up in a helicopter before and jumped at the chance. It was marvellous. Each trip lasted about 20 minutes or so, and took guests, six or seven at a time, out to sea, back over the bay and then over the mountains. It was truly awesome. However, two of the ladies in my party were more than a little nervous and looked decidedly apprehensive to say the least as we waited in random groups for our turn to climb aboard the craft. One of the more colourful larger than life characters of my party, he had been the manager of a well known Irish football team, sensing their predicament, had been loudly talking about the chances of a crash, adding that he was glad that he had just updated his will and that his affairs were all in order. But still the two ladies went ahead.

Just as the door closed on us and it was too late to get out, he called out to them in a light-hearted effort to reassure them, relieve the tension or to wind them up even further, "I was only joking with you. Anyway it is very safe. Honest it is." He added for good measure, "We will be alright...quite safe...after all we have the Reverend with us. Nothing will happen to us, God will see to that." I could not resist the urge to reply just after the helicopter left the ground that this could be God's way of getting rid of me. It did go rather quiet for a bit, but we made it safely back to the extensive grounds of this beautiful hotel without any

129

trouble at all. One lady was still clutching her rosary beads and muttering her prayers as we climbed out. She placed her feet firmly on the ground and walked off in the direction of the bar.

The wedding rehearsal and the bomb blast

The evening Alex was blown out of bed, or claimed to be, was the most dramatic event of all the wedding experiences, by far. I had left the family at home for a normal evening, a bit of TV, a bath and then to bed. I went into the church and started to prepare. I met, greeted and chatted with the stream of visitors and well wishers, and waited until all of the necessary participants were present. I then explained in great and solemn detail all that would happen on the day, from beginning to end. I dealt with the usual questions and requests. All was going very well, indeed. My rehearsal patter was genuine, but it was in itself a well-rehearsed routine. We then got to the bit where we were ready to do the walkthrough, the bit where all the key players are at their stations and ready to go and we would literally walk through the whole thing. I went to the church door with the bride and her full entourage: maid of honour, bridesmaids and pageboys, the full set. We proceeded as if the bride had just arrived at the church for the real thing, and slowly made our way to the front of the church, right by the Communion Table, me leading them as I would do on the day itself to ensure she did not rush madly up the aisle fuelled by nervous energy. It has been seen, and this entrance has to be dignified.

We arrived at the front of the church where the groom to be and the best man and ushers awaited us. With everyone in place, I began to talk them through the words which would when done in full in a few days time to cement them together as husband and wife. It was all going very well. When suddenly there was a tremendous and terrifying explosion. The whole building shook. It literally seemed that the church roof lifted up and then dropped back into place again. At the same moment of impact the church doors blew open with a loud bang. It was an awful and truly frightening moment.

It was at this moment that Alex, who had been asleep in the manse, came down the stairs to find Angela to tell her she had been blown out of bed.

Back in the church, the groom, who had been rather nervous during the whole procedure, was as white as a sheet. I am sure that he was fine about getting married, but I think the enormity of the day and being centre stage had begun to terrify him. His face when the doors were thrown open with a tremendous force was ashen. He went white. Mind you his reaction was mirrored on most of the faces gathered there, the look of shock and fear. It was a sound most of the people had heard many times before. It was a huge explosion and the all too familiar sound and aftershock of a bomb, closely followed by an eerie silence and then the hushed uncertainty descended.

We all looked at one another. "That was very close," whispered one man, "very close indeed." Another responded, "Aye, too close." Afterwards, a number of the people told me that they feared that the nearby hotel had been targeted again. The Lancaster Hotel had been the victim of an IRA bomb attack several years before. A number of people had died. It had been a mistake, or so I was told by some in my congregation, in that the intended victims were policemen and women and somehow a mistake had been made for that night it was not a gathering of police, it was a gathering of dog breeders. Many of my congregation had been working at the hotel at the time or had relatives working there, some of whom had been injured or killed. The memories were still raw. Some of my congregation currently worked there. The immediate thought for many was, "Oh God, not the Lancaster again."

We all made our way warily out of the church and waited. The big fear was always what was going to happen next. In the dark, recent history of Northern Ireland there had been a custom of setting off another bomb quickly after the first in order to cause havoc amongst the police and soldiers gathering to deal with the aftermath of the first explosion. We were still unsure where the bomb had been placed.

It turned out that a truck carrying over 2000lbs of explosives had been parked near to the Forensic Science Laboratory at Castlereagh, about 3 miles away. It was said to be the largest bomb ever used in Northern Ireland. It damaged hundreds and hundreds of houses and a church. I still have pictures of the damaged buildings, taken next day. It was a miracle that no one was injured or killed thanks to an early warning phone call and the security forces clearing the area. The Laboratory which was responsible for providing much forensic evidence in the fight against terrorism was destroyed.

The incident was reported in *The Independent*, two days later, Friday 25th of September 1992, with the following headline:

Damage in huge blast put at 20m pounds: A Belfast housing estate counts the cost of an IRA bomb which may have destroyed vital criminal evidence

David McKittrick the paper's Ireland Correspondent, wrote this:

The IRA bomb which wrecked the forensic science laboratory on the outskirts of Belfast was one of the biggest detonated in a residential area of Northern Ireland. The 2,000lb (900kg) device reduced every room to rubble. It also caused damage, in some cases severe, to more than 700 homes and other premises. One estimate put repair costs after the blast at about pounds 20m.

The wrecking of the laboratory late on Wednesday night is a blow to the authorities, because the blast may well have destroyed valuable forensic evidence for use in the prosecution of terrorist suspects. But on a personal level it was a traumatic night for hundreds of families who lived through the explosion and face the task of repairing their homes.

The blast was unusually loud and destructive. It shook Belfast and was heard for miles around. Many people living some distance away were convinced the explosion had been outside their door. One man who lives 10 miles away thought his home was under attack and went outside with a golf club to investigate.

Emergency staff said the area affected was one of the largest they had ever known, with damage reported up to a radius of a mile and a half. But the brunt of the damage was suffered by Belvoir Park, a largely Protestant housing estate separated from the laboratory by a dual carriageway. Up to 50 homes may have to be demolished. Belvoir Park, has been a model and almost incident-free housing estate, built by a public authority, but is now largely privately owned. In one experience which is typical of many, a 65-year-old widow who lives alone was watching television when the bomb went off. Much of the plaster ceiling collapsed while the window shattered into fragments and showered the room. An immediate power cut plunged the house into darkness. She escaped with only a slight cut to the head.

After the explosion people roamed the darkened estate in cars and on foot, checking for relatives and friends while police officers helped tend those suffering from shock and injuries. No one was seriously hurt. A number of pet cats and dogs panicked and ran off into the night. In the early hours of the morning rain poured through damaged roofs, making life even more difficult for families involved in immediate repair work. At 5am, almost eight hours after the blast, workmen were still engaged in boarding up broken windows.

Very early next morning I went straight to the area, which was about three miles from the manse and well into the outskirts of Belfast. Quite a few of my congregation had been affected with damage to their homes and smashed windows, and so on. Surveying the scene soon confirmed it was one of total devastation, and made it clear that the press reports filtering through, and the local gossip which arrived even more quickly, were in no way exaggerations. It really was a miracle that no one was killed that night. Hundreds of people were badly affected though, and the shock and fear lasted long after the shoring up of broken homes to make them as safe as possible, until the rebuilding programme got underway. Some, as I understand it, were never able to return to their homes.

****

Standing outside the Moneymore Church seconds after the explosion that night , with the echo of it seeming still to hang heavily in the air, or at least still ringing in our ears, we looked at one another, not knowing exactly what had happened or where. We only knew that it was a big one and that it was close, as the man said. We called it a night and people quickly left for home, safety and to catch the news reports as they broke.

I did the same. Wondering what had happened, who or how many had been affected and how might it affect my congregation. I also spared a thought for the poor bride and groom. Not the best way to end your wedding rehearsal.

It turned out that neither the groom, nor the bride, took this to be a bad omen for their forthcoming marriage. The following Saturday the wedding took place as arranged. There was still an air of fear around. Looking back at the experience, and reading the above newspaper account of the drama, I now wonder why we were so disbelieving of Alex. I think it caught us all by surprise. We were not used to this sort of thing. Alex had come downstairs to Angela, who perhaps thought Alex was exaggerating and maybe even finding an excuse for not staying in bed; it had been known. Most likely Angela wanted to play down the whole thing so as not to scare the children, who seemed more puzzled than frightened by the experience. When I came in some 15 or 20 minutes after seeing off the last of the wedding party and locking up the church, we played it all down and took the children back to bed. Next morning we teased Alex that she had probably dreamt that she had been turned out of bed by the explosion. It all sounded too dramatic. Over the years, in spite of her maintaining that it was true, the teasing continued. Looking back our reaction was one of disbelief and a way of dealing with it. I now suspect Alex was right all along. My apologies now go out to Alex in a most public way through this book: Alex, we believe you.

A long and bloody history and, too close to home, the atrocity at Loughinisland

I referred earlier to the terrible tragedy of the Loughinisland massacre. This was terror on a huge scale, involving not rival sectarian factions who were themselves causing terror, maiming and slaughtering for their cause, but innocent people. I am not sure we could find an example of a more innocent group of people: villagers of all ages gathering together for the joy of sharing a football match on TV in the local pub. Loughinisland seemed to be such a safe place, a sleepy village on the very outskirts of Downpatrick, famous only for the nearby church ruins which date back to the 13th century. Now infamous for the night of devastation caused by two masked gunmen as part of the growing tit-for-tat killings, the ever increasing spiral of violence generated by the increasing talks for peace and political agreement. Sectarian factions on both "sides" it seems were threatened by the possibility that there would be a peace agreement and they would lose out, politically, on land, or power.

We were outsiders to the whole thing, but heard lots of accounts of what really fuelled the Troubles. It was evident to us that most of the people we met wanted only to get on with their lives safely, to live in peace, and that the Troubles were perpetuated by a powerful minority. Some valued these unofficial guardians of the people, claiming they gave more protection from the "other side" than the security forces offered, seen in the way they were said to deal with drug dealers or suspected child abusers, or the joy riders who blighted the Province at that time. Punishment was swift, sharp and painful, usually involving a bullet in the knee cap or a "double," a bullet in both. Some claimed that the terrorists on both sides were nothing more than Kray-style gangsters and extortionists, raking off huge sums of money from the construction and leisure industries, the building sites, pubs and clubs, and so on. Many stories were told to us about someone who knew someone who was only allowed to operate his bar or building site if he paid large sums of money every month to the local terrorist group or mafia as they called them.

There was a much wider backcloth to consider in that the history of Ireland seems to have been one of a long and bloody conflict for hundreds of years. The modern period seems to have started with the success of King Billy (William III of Orange) over James II at the battle of the Boyne in 1693. The events of which are kept alive in the popular mind by the wall murals depicting the victorious King Billy on his white horse – the champion of the Ulster Protestants. These can be contrasted with the "Brits Out" murals in other areas. Each year the Orange Lodge Parades made sure no one would forget. I had mixed feelings about the parades and incurred the wrath of some of my congregation when I questioned the need for the minister to be seen to support them. This may have been the beginning of the end of my ministry in Northern Ireland, as I was expected to support these parades fully.

139

I am still not qualified to offer an opinion about the rights and wrong of the historic land claims or the rights to political power. I wonder who is. Certainly no one from the outside was my feeling, no one who had been born elsewhere and had not lived through the terrible atrocities which have scarred and shaped the minds of so many. It seemed to me that the best way forward was to forget the past and to move on looking for a positive future for all. It was not that simple. A considerable minority on each side of the divide were vehemently and passionately against any kind of co-operation with the other side, and were locked in a fearful impasse and resisted any move to give up an inch of land or to make political progress towards reconciliation. We were told that the breeding grounds for the terrorists on both sides of the divide were the poor working class areas where unemployment was high and prospects low. Here young people could find money, power, status and fame, or infamy, by joining and climbing the ranks of the illegal terrorist organisation which governed their community: the IRA, or other splinter groups on the Republican side, or the UDA, UFF, UDF on the loyalist side. Being loyal here meant loyalty to the Queen and the Union, and the continued rule from Parliament, London. One thing we gathered was that this war, for this is what it was in reality for many, a war, was not about religion. The religious wars of the past were no longer a feature of cultural life as they once were. However, religion, it seemed, had been hijacked and used as a way of stirring up people's emotions and was a handy and additional way of classifying people into two opposing groups: Roman Catholics/Republicans on the one side, who were said to want a united Ireland and

140

the "Brits [British troops] Out," who gathered under the Tricolour, the Republic of Ireland flag. On the other side, those who gathered under the red, white and blue of the Union Jack, who marched on the 12th of July at the Orange Parade, the unionists, Protestant, loyalists.

****

We never could really claim to understand the issues. We knew that there had been a long, long history of conflict and bloodshed, going back for hundreds of years. We knew that the recent events, the modern day Troubles, so to speak, stemmed from the mid-1960s and early 1970s onwards. A time from which brutal and bloody scenes had been commonplace on, at times dominating, our TV screens in England as I was growing up. We did know that the conflict had claimed many, many lives from the time Home Secretary James Callaghan sent in the troops, the British Army, on the 14th of August 1969, in a move to prevent a civil war. The BBC, *On this Day* reports it like this:

1969: British troops sent into Northern Ireland

The British Government has sent troops into Northern Ireland in what it says is a "limited operation" to restore law and order. It follows three days and two nights of violence in the mainly-Catholic Bogside area of Londonderry. Trouble has also erupted in Belfast and other towns across Northern Ireland.

It also comes after a speech by the Prime Minister of the Irish Republic, Jack Lynch, regarded by many as "outrageous interference" in which he called for a United Nations peacekeeping force to be sent to the Province. He also called for Anglo-Irish talks on the future of Northern Ireland.

The Prime Minister of Northern Ireland, Major James Chichester-Clark, responded by saying neighbourly relations with the Republic were at an end and that British troops were being called in. The British Home Secretary James Callaghan was in a plane on his way to talks with Prime Minister Harold Wilson in Cornwall when he received a radio-telephone call asking for troops to be deployed.

Shortly after 1700 hours local time, 300 troops from the 1st Battalion, Prince of Wales's Own Regiment of Yorkshire, occupied the centre of Londonderry, replacing the exhausted police officers who had been patrolling the cordons around the Bogside.

It is said that over 3250 lives have been claimed since then.

****

142

A number of my congregation who referred to the day the troops were sent in expressed the view that it would have been much better for the British government not to have interfered, leaving the people to sort it out for themselves. It might have been a bloodbath, one man told me, but it would have "sorted things out once and for all." I was shocked to hear this and equally shocked to read in the national newspapers early in January of 1994 that the UDA had released a document calling for a re-partition of Northern Ireland complete, with "Ethnic cleansing," it was said, in an attempt to make a new and smaller Northern Ireland wholly Protestant.

The "Doomsday Plan," as it became known, was to be implemented should the British Army ever withdraw from Northern Ireland. The mostly Irish Catholic and nationalist areas would be handed over to the Republic, and those left stranded in the "Protestant State" would be "Expelled, nullified, or interned."

Even now, Angela and I can never really claim to have understood the Troubles, nor to have a real insight into what really motivated the people who carried out the atrocities, or those who simply showed their colours and their prejudices when the chips were down. It is far too complex for a simple historical survey to reveal the truth. It seemed to be terribly complicated and involve deep rooted psychological and sociological factors and fears and the need to belong, protect and survive. All of these deeply human drives and passions were played out against and within the brutal and unforgiving setting of a long and bloody history of conflict.

It would take a much greater mind than mine to unravel that lot, I often thought. We could never really understand it, and somehow felt we had only just scratched the surface in our five years there. It was not for us to comment or condemn. After all we were outsiders, and at times it felt like it, seemingly coming from a different world. All I could do as minister, an influential and representative figure, was to try to be understanding, reasonable and compassionate, and I could try to encourage my congregation to be the same. Whilst I did not claim to have real insight into the Troubles, I did see the devastation at first hand.

****

The Loughinisland massacre occurred, as I explained above, on the night of the Republic of Ireland's football game against Italy in the 1994 World Cup Finals. The tiny, sleepy village of Loughinisland was devastated. The two masked men who ran into the bar with machine guns left behind them a trail of devastation: eight people were killed and many were injured, many of them seriously. The survivors, and I presume the dead, were taken to Downpatrick Hospital some four miles away. I know the survivors were taken there because the word came through on the grapevine. The whole town was in a state of shock.

There had been tragedies in the area before, of course. We were told of the time in recent memory when a roadside bomb was detonated by a terrorist hidden in long grass high up in the fields above just as a group of soldiers were walking past on a patrol, killing all six. This spot was then marked for years by a continually renewed floral tribute consisting of several wreaths and floral displays. The colourful, visual reminder meant people could hardly fail to remember the event as they drove past. There was the shooting and killing of Margaret's brother (Margaret was my Church Warden), and the shooting of the IRA member in the local park, just at the back of our second manse. It was chilling to set off for a casual Sunday afternoon walk with our young children over to the park so close to our home and suddenly come across a wooden memorial cross with the inscription: In the memory of an IRA member, "killed", it said, "by the British," whilst on "active service." We understand that on the day in question he had shot at a passing police patrol in the town and had been chased into the park and shot dead.

Downpatrick was not without its share of the Troubles. It was only 18 miles south of Belfast and many of its people worked in the city and had over the years become accustomed to the disruption caused by regular bomb scares or bomb hoaxes, which brought the city to a standstill. The town itself did suffer regular terrorist attacks on the heavily fortressed, grey, steel fence and barbed wire protected police station. Our manse was just along the road and we were very concerned that a misguided mortar bomb would miss its target, the police station, and land on our

145

house. Likewise, our concerns over the police and Army roadblocks which regularly turned up and positioned themselves on St Patrick's Avenue, right outside our manse. These checkpoints were also regularly subjected to attacks from snipers or mortar bombs. All of this was a bit too close to home for comfort.

We were never comfortable when we saw the Army and police trucks arrive and set themselves up for the checks on motorists passing through town, complete with their own gunmen at the ready, perhaps behind a parked car, or in a front garden, crouched behind a bush or tree, with rifle to eye scanning the scene before them, on red alert, as their colleagues did the checking of the car occupants and details. We were always very relieved when they pulled out. They, too, must have felt very vulnerable. We did. Especially since a number of the mortar attacks were bungled or landed in the wrong place. Nevertheless, Downpatrick seemed to be a reasonably peaceful place to live. Indeed, after the fairly insular rural community on the edge of Belfast of our first congregation, this was an enlightened place.

It was a predominately Roman Catholic town, but had achieved a remarkable sharing of political power and the people lived in delicate harmony. The dynamics were fascinating to us in that a town with a population of some 20,000, only 20%, we were told, were Protestant; so, a rare Protestant minority in Northern Ireland, where overall the Roman Catholic population was approximately one third of the one-and-a-half-million people. It was, of course, the

Town of St Patrick and claimed to be the Saint's town, the place where he first arrived and the place of his burial. There were others claiming the same for other places, but this did not daunt the townspeople of Downpatrick or the Tourist Board from making St Patrick their very own.

It was generally a place of relative peace, even if the local Protestant newsagent received a bullet through the post, and the local Protestant undertaker received a wreath, following the events of the Loughinisland massacre.

****

Downpatrick was not without its share of the Troubles, but nothing like the night the two Protestant paramilitaries stormed into the quiet village bar where the locals were gathered to watch their national team play a game of football in the World Cup Finals.

The news soon spread. People rang me and called at the manse, "Had I heard?" They were very distressed and frightened. When the news broke first in sketchy detail very late that evening on TV and radio, it was hard to believe. It was like watching a film, a fiction, portraying the worst and darkest side of human nature. It couldn't be true. This could not be happening in this quiet and sleepy village on the outskirts of this seemingly peaceful and happy town. The town which seemed to accommodate quite happily people of both religious and political persuasions, living side by side, sharing the same shops and library, sports centre and racetrack. Most people shared the same desire to get on with life and the challenges of everyday living: the school run, paying the bills and looking after the family. There was a huge sense of unreality about the whole thing as we watched the drama unfold on television and heard the responses in radio interviews. We did not sleep much that night. It was not the first or last time we talked, or tossed and turned, throughout the night.

The massacre and what to do next?

Very early next morning, as the papers were already proclaiming the tragedy in bold print, I popped out to see my nearby neighbour, a Church of Ireland cleric. A strange hush had descended on the town. There were few people around. The usual early morning dog walkers were not to be seen. There were hardly any cars. The people who were visible hurried, heads down, to their destinations. No one made eye contact, at least with me.

I felt that given I was a Protestant minister in a predominately Roman Catholic town, I ought to do something. At very least I should offer some gesture of support. After all, I was a representative figure. I represented not only my church congregation, but on occasions like this I represented the Protestant community. And, understandably, tensions would be high. But I was not sure what to do. I spoke to my neighbour who was a very experienced minister. He said that all the clerics of the town should gather at his house at 9.00am. So it was that the morning after the atrocity I met with my local Protestant minister colleagues. We all had a very good working relationship, and often shared in special services in the town like Remembrance Day and Christmas Eve vigils, and so on, with, I might add, the Roman Catholic clergy.

We duly assembled. I was very surprised when there was a cautious reluctance at the meeting. I, as a comparatively young and inexperienced minister, and effectively an outsider to the ways of the Province, was keen to attend the funerals which would take place over the next few days. This was not well received; in hindsight they were probably right. They had far more experience than I did, and I was then rather idealistic in my approach. Perhaps our presence at a time when emotions were so heightened would have been too much and sparked another atrocity. It would only take one hothead. Instead the agreement was that we, the four of us representing the different Protestant churches, should visit the Presbytery, the house of the Roman Catholic priests of Loughinisland, to offer our support. And so we did. We climbed into one car and drove the short distance, through the winding lanes to Loughinisland. There was not much to it: farms, an odd house, here and there, a shop, the Roman Catholic Church (or Chapel as the Roman Catholic place of worship was called by Protestants to distinguish it from their own churches, possibly reflecting it as secondary or nonconformist) and the Presbytery, where the priests lived. Here it was the four of us presented ourselves, representing our Protestant community.

****

I should have said that as we approached the village, the country lane was thronged with people, people just

150

standing there, in silence or whispering to one another. It was something I had noticed on other occasions, for example that day on the Shankill Road. Whenever a tragedy struck large groups of people gathered, lost, bewildered and fearful of what might come next, as if there was some safety in numbers, perhaps not knowing what else to do, some herding instinct seemed to take over and the people left their homes and gathered together.

Our driver had to slow down to a crawl to make our way safely past the gathered throngs lining the way to the Presbytery. It was quite disconcerting and in the car we all felt a growing unease and tension. It was obvious from our clerical garb who we were and who we represented. In any case we were well known local figures. In Northern Ireland at the time the ministers held powerful local offices, featured heavily in local events and in the local press. I, for example, was a governor of a local school and sat on the governing committee of the ACE scheme, a scheme training and paying over 80 long-term unemployed local people to do gardening and decorating and so on for the elderly by way of rehabilitating them and training them for full-time work.

It was obvious who we were. You had only to open the local newspaper to see our faces at some fete or meeting some dignitary or at some local or regional event. On one occasion I had been pictured being introduced to Mary Robinson, the new President of the Republic of Ireland, on her visit to Downpatrick, the County Town of Down. Around this time a well known TV personality came to the town, for

151

what purpose I cannot recall, and I was invited to meet him. For some reason, I think it was to do with the Tourist Board and the launch of a cultural centre, there was Irish Dancing. I still have the press-cutting of this celebrity with three or four town dignitaries and me, all lined up, arms linked, with each of us holding one leg up in the air in a fake Irish dancing pose, all looking faintly ridiculous. Riverdance it was not

****

There was no doubt that all of the occupants of the car were well known to the good people of Downpatrick and Loughinisland. Yes, the people who lined the lanes knew who we were and turned to stare at us as we made our way slowly to the Presbytery. An eerie silence descended and followed our progress. We parked at the foot of a long drive, climbed out and made our way through the crowds up to the front door of the priests' house. We rang the bell in silence. It was a very tense few moments. I now began to understand the earlier reluctance of my colleagues. We all were relieved when the front door opened and we were let in to the relative security of the priests' house. We were ushered into a large hall and then shown into a large front room where sat several priests. Some were known to us, others were not. Formal introductions were made and it was, to be honest, a rather frosty and tense reception. This was perhaps understandable.

We chatted to the senior priest and offered our sincere and heartfelt sadness at such terrible events. This was accepted. It was agreed that our presence at the forthcoming funerals would not be a helpful or good thing. We had tea.

We left in silence and made our way through the crowds to the car and set off slowly towards home. The people simply stared. They were lost and hurting. Many in such a small community had lost a relative or friend. In such a place everyone knew everyone, and when tragedy struck it struck each and everyone of the community. There was an old saying we heard time and time again, "Kick one and they all bleed." That night all the people of Loughinisland were bleeding and weeping.

We returned home. Our final conversation was to express the unease we all had felt and the relief that we were home safely. I asked what my colleague would do next, if anything. There was silence. As I left them and walked the short distance home, my head reeling at the events of the past 14 hours or so, I decided that I would do something more. After all, I was Chaplain to the hospital where the survivors and the dead, had been taken. There was something more I could do even if my colleagues felt it unwise. I decided that there was only one right course of action. I decided that I should go and meet the survivors.

Meeting the survivors of a bleeding and weeping but unbroken community

I went into the manse, sat and had a cup of tea and talked through my visit to the priests' house in Loughinisland with Angela and told her of my plan. Rightly so, she was very concerned. The horror of the events was unfolding by the hour, as more and more news was released of the number dead and injured. Everyone in the community was shocked, horrified and frightened by the events and the possibility of what might happen next. Everyone was only too aware of the chilling and unpredictable cycle of violence which had been spiralling out of control over the past weeks. The victims of this latest travesty were all Roman Catholics and this fact and this alone had been enough for the crazed gunmen on a mission.

The Protestant population of Downpatrick were a minority (some 20% of the population I was told). What had been a happy power-sharing town could easily change. The temperature could rise dramatically and reprisals against Protestants begin. Not here in Downpatrick, people said, but they were, I felt, unconvinced by their own words trying to reassure me and themselves. After all, on the outskirts of this town was the Flying Horse Estate, a huge council estate comprised of low-rise blocks of flats and houses. It was said to be under the control of and a breeding ground for the IRA. The tricolour flew from many poles and balconies. I was told that the police or Army would only enter this estate in combat ready groups, such was the potential danger.

This was the estate I had to walk slowly past at the head of a funeral: leading the cortege, coffin, hearses and scores of mourners for over two miles from an outlying home, past this estate and into Downpatrick and to the church for burial. I was certainly hot under the collar as I led this Protestant funeral party slowly and with dignity, with me walking two or three yards ahead of the coffin bearers, sweating profusely; past the flats and the tricolours of the notorious Flying Horse Estate and on towards town. I was told by an angry Protestant mourner that these flags were illegal, but the police were too scared to go in there and take them down.

****

It would not have been unrealistic to expect a backlash on the Protestant community immediately following the Loughinisland massacre. No wonder my Protestant community were frightened. Angela had the additional worry of me. She knew that I would do what I thought was right, even if it was foolhardy. I had never been overly concerned about my own safety when it came down to what I considered to be the right and wrongs of life.

This attitude was evident about three years earlier when I went alone to Transylvania in the west of Romania, to try to adopt an orphan after seeing all of the terrible pictures in the press of the unwanted children of Ceausescu's regime, abandoned to the orphanages by parents who could not afford to keep them. This entailed a dangerous journey on a night train across Romania at a time when law and order were minimal following the collapse of Ceausescu's rule. I was unsuccessful and had one or two near misses, but I had never been put off by the possible danger when I felt something was the right thing to do.

The same spirit had led me to spend some time helping at the Four Homes of Mercy many years before; this was a Palestinian home for severely disabled Arab people at Bethany, just on the outskirts of Jerusalem, on the edge of the desert. This was another adventure, which held its own risks from desert dogs, scorpions and bandits, especially as I was sleeping alone in a hut on the edge of the desert. Even staying with an Arab community was greatly frowned upon by the Israeli authorities, as I found when I tried to explain the nature of my visit as I entered the country at a time of high security and tension.

It was this same spirit which had led me to take up the challenge to go to Northern Ireland for my first ministry. After all, Lebanon was not a real possibility. And now I decided that the right thing to do, even if it was deemed unwise and provocative by some to attend the victim's funerals, was to visit the survivors; after all I was a representative figure and Chaplain to the hospital where they were being treated. Angela was, as ever, unstinting in her support.

****

I made my way there. It was merely a five-minute walk. I walked slowly and ponderously. Once again there were crowds of hushed and distressed people in the car park and gathered outside the main entrance; they were not sure what to do next. I made my way through them and found a similar scene inside. The reception area was full to overflowing, as were the corridors. I made my way towards a familiar face: a senior member of staff, with whom I regularly chatted during my visiting, which could be three or four or more times a week. I explained why I had come and he took me through to the wards.

Lining the corridors to the wards were trolleys and equipment and relatives and friends of the victims. It felt like a war zone. There had obviously been frantic activity overnight and still it continued. The relatives waited anxiously for news of their loved ones. The staff looked tired, drawn and some were red-eyed and tearful. In a small tight-knit community, most if not all of the staff knew the victims or had friends who did. All were wounded and bleeding as a result of the two gunmen with what they

157

thought was a cause. The big question I wanted to pose to the two was this: was any cause, real or imaginary, worth this?

****

I was led past the relatives and into one of the small rooms where the first of the victims I was to meet, a man, was propped up in the hospital bed, attached to the usual equipment and paraphernalia one usually sees at the bedside of someone who is undergoing serious hospital treatment; there were wires and tubes and lots of activity from the very attentive doctors and nurses who were dressing his wounds. I stood quietly alongside. He glanced up and nodded his recognition of me and my presence. I bowed my head and prayed silently. Then I moved on to another room.

****

That morning I visited several people, all with their permission and the permission of the hospital staff. I certainly did not want my presence to be a source of stress or irritation or to get in the way of the hospital routine. In my experience hospital staff were always fantastic at accommodating me as a minister, making every effort to give me quality time with my congregant, their patient. It was as if most of them were very aware of the spiritual dimension of a patient's well-being, especially at the most serious times, at times of crisis. I recall once being ushered into a lift with the hospital orderly, who was pushing a patient down to operating theatre for a serious operation. My visit to the hospital had coincided, quite coincidentally, at the time the staff were preparing this lady for her operation; and she was petrified. She asked me to pray for her, and I did. She clasped my hand.

A nurse accompanied us as we left the ward and made our way to the lifts which were signed with the dreaded:

"TO THEATRES

HOSPITAL STAFF ONLY"

As we reached the lift the nurse firmly but kindly told the relatives who trailed behind the bed to, "Stay here," as relatives were not allowed beyond this point. "Come on Father," she said to me, and I was ushered into the lift, the lady still clutching my hand for grim death. Several floors below the lift stopped, the lift door opened and I was allowed into the ante-room, with the main swing doors to "Theatre Two" flapping open each time the theatre staff made their way in and out, busily carrying out their duties. I spoke to the lady again assuring her that she was in very good hands and would be fine. Mine was the last voice she heard as the nurse inserted the cannula and administered the drugs which took her into a deep sleep. My job done, I returned to wait with the worried relatives until the operation was successfully over.

****

The rest of the day after the shooting at Loughinisland was spent at the hospital. It was more a case of being a visible presence rather than what I could say (we all recognize that sometimes words are wholly inadequate). I did speak to those who were less seriously injured and their families and I was well received. One or two would not look at me, but this may have been due to shock and the horror of it all, rather than any sectarian bias. Some of the victims had wounds to their legs. It was later suggested to me that either the bullets had been sprayed low, or the injured had thrown themselves down to the floor and their flailing legs had been caught in the stream of fire. I am not sure.

The wounds I saw whilst they were being dressed were horrific. I also spoke to a number of the hospital staff, some of whom I had got to know during my time as Chaplain to the hospital. All were deeply shocked and many had worked though the night and all of the next day treating the many that had been affected. They had worked on stoically, in spite of having to deal with their own feelings often in the knowledge that people they knew personally were dead or badly injured. It was a trying time for all. I left feeling drained and empty. I remember asking myself on the way home to the manse, Angela and my children, "What sort of place is this?"

Back in the Manse, a day off which went wrong: a BBQ, and nearly caught on the beer

In spite of these dreadful and sadly regular atrocities, family life in the manse carried on as normal; well as normal as it could be given the life of a minister. The children went to school and socialised with friends. We went out as a family as often as we could given the huge demands placed upon me. We watched TV and had BBQs in the manse garden, although we felt we had to be careful not to be seen drinking alcohol. As I have mentioned in several places, not only did we enjoy a drink, at times it seemed to be a life-saver as we returned home after a particularly trying event: the visit to Sharon and Ben's, for example, or as we sat and pondered what we had got ourselves into, or what to do next in any particular situation. It is perhaps a great wonder that we did not end up with a dependency problem. Of course we had to restrict our intake not only because we had a young family, but also because we were never quite sure who would turn up at the manse unexpected and unannounced.

We were told many times that many of the congregation were vehemently against alcohol. It was, I think, a hangover from the old Puritan ways. There was a degree of superiority about it all, especially when we were told that the dirty "Taigs," the insulting slang used for Roman Catholics, were all drunkards. There was a degree of hypocrisy too. We knew of many of the congregation who did "take drink," as it was put, but would make sure they were never seen to do so in public. In fact the day I broke my 24-hour fast for charity (raising money for the Sudan appeal) three senior members of my congregation celebrated with me in a most untypical way in the manse, partaking with me in the remnants of several bottles of spirits they had brought round in a large cardboard box. There was a good choice: half a bottle of whiskey, a quarter bottle of vodka, half a bottle of sweet sherry, a dribble of gin and so on. We polished off the lot. Not a good idea after a 24-hour fast.

This made counting the piles of notes and coins at the kitchen table a bit of a farce. It turned into a very complicated and protracted affair. Each count threw up a different grand total, with the totals varying hugely in proportion to the alcohol consumed. By the fifth or sixth attempt, there was over £2000, mostly in coins, many of which ended up on the floor, we gave up and agreed that we would hand it into the bank the next day and let the experts do it.

This celebration would not have met with the approval of my predecessor who was vehemently anti-alcohol to the point of obsession. This man famously flounced out of a church meeting because someone had passed to him, I suspect deliberately out of mischief, a liquor chocolate. He

163

apparently bit into it without checking what it was, thinking it was an ordinary chocolate, and when the taste of Tia Maria oozed over his tongue he spat it out onto the hall floor and stomped off in a "hissy-fit" shouting that he would never again trust his congregation. The congregation members present were split between those who fell about laughing and those who were very concerned that "His Reverence" had been mortally offended. The next time they met the minister made no reference to his unfortunate flirtation with alcohol; neither did the members of the congregation. The least said the soonest mended. He most certainly would not have approved of my celebration with some senior members of my congregation that evening to mark the end of my 24-hour fast and shut-in in the church. I am not sure that my head appreciated it next morning, either.

****

One sunny day we decided I would take a few hours off and we would have a BBQ. We would try to pretend that we were a normal family enjoying a normal life, without interruption. We invited a family with whom we had become good friends. I got to know Seamus through studying for a higher degree at the University of Ulster. He was a smashing chap, and we initially met up on the first evening of the part-time course and then shared the drive each week to the campus a few miles north of Belfast, at

Jordanstown, or the much longer hike up to Coleraine, some 100 miles of a round trip. This was an awful journey on a Friday evening. The course took place from 5.00pm to 8.00pm. I will never understand who devised this arrangement, or why, unless it was out of a general mischievousness or bitterness.

The outward journey to Coleraine took two or three hours as we had to cross Belfast at rush-hour. The return journey took about 90 minutes. On these journeys I had the chance to get to know Seamus very well. He was a teacher, the Head of a Religious Studies Department at a secondary school in Belfast. Seamus had a lovely wife, Roisin, and two delightful children, Bryony and Sarah. They were a lovely family and we became firm friends. We tried to see them as often as our busy work schedules would allow, which unfortunately was not that often. It was healthy for us to have friends outside of the congregation; indeed, we were warned it was not advisable to have friends as such amongst the congregation. This was a pity because there were some fantastic people amongst the church members.

So we were delighted to meet and become friends with the likes of Seamus and Roisin. As I have said they were delightful; there was only one problem, not a problem for Angela or I, of course, or for Seamus and Roisin, but a problem for some. You see Seamus and Roisin and their children, as you may have worked out from their names, were not a "good, 'clean-living' Protestant family," they were horror of horrors, Roman Catholic. It had not really crossed our minds that there would be a problem, but we should have known. We had socialized at Seamus and Roisin's home several times; they had visited our home, the manse, a number of times; but no member of our congregation had met them. The manse was large enough to accommodate any number of visitors without them necessarily meeting up. We had that grand front room which had become my study on one side at the front of this large double-fronted house. On this occasion it was different.

****

We had set the BBQ in the most private corner of the garden going. Inside we were chopping the vegetables for the skewers, wrapping the potatoes in foil and making spicy oil with which to soak the skewers, when there was a knock on the door. In came Linda, a late middle-aged member of the congregation. Linda was one of the nicest, kindest, most generously spirited people you could wish to meet. She had really taken to our children and they to her. She was very charity minded and was generous in her giving to all of the many and impressive church fundraising efforts and to the church itself. Linda came in and warmly embraced us and the children and said hello to our guests. She cooed over the two visiting children, "Look at the wee darlings." Then she asked, "What are their names?" This is "Bryony and this is Sarah," I said, "and this is Mum and Dad, Seamus and Roisin."

166

We were staggered at the instant and dramatic change which came over Linda's face. It was as if we had introduced her to the very devil himself, complete with horns, red smoke and tail. Linda, who usually stayed for a very long time, sometimes too long, chatting and telling us the latest news of the church members or news from the "country folk" (meaning the goings on and gossip in the immediate farming area and surrounding villages). Not on this occasion. This day, Linda hastily explained to us, almost over her shoulder as she hurried down the hall, that she was in a great rush and had so many things to do, and that Mrs Macleery was waiting for her to call to take her shopping, and so on. With that the front door banged shut. It seems that we had committed a cardinal sin by having Roman Catholics in the manse.

Our guests just looked at us and shrugged. It seems that it did not faze them at all. It appears they had seen it all before. They were not in the least bit offended and carried on like nothing had happened. We were very shocked and more than a little hurt and felt somewhat let down. After all, this was a church. We were claiming to be Christians. Where was the room for this kind of attitude? Shocked as we were at this, the day did not get any better. Worse was to come.

****

At the start of the day of the BBQ, all had seemed well: a rare day off, a sunny day as well, a day with the family, a day with friends. How normal could you get? Then the Linda issue, followed by two more experiences which put an even larger and darker shadow over the day, adding to the unpleasant taste left by the hasty and pointed retreat of Linda. This was not due to the weather as unusually for Northern Ireland the day was a lovely, sunny, warm one. These clouds came from within the manse.

After Linda had gone, we carried on not mentioning it again, finishing off preparing all the items we needed for the BBQ, including some vegetarian sausages which were not easily found in Northern Ireland at that time. I spent the customary hour or so trying to get the briquettes to light and finally did what we are not supposed to do. There must be some primal urge connected to fire which propels us on to do this with BBQs in spite of all the warnings. I smothered them in petrol. This worked a treat, though I admit it was a stupid thing to do. When they were glowing red-hot, I put the food on to cook.

We had anguished about whether we should have any alcohol with our BBQ as the manse garden was very exposed. We could easily be seen from the street unless we positioned ourselves very carefully away from prying eyes; even then if anyone cared to walk down the drive towards the garage we would immediately come into their view after a few paces. The drive to the garage ran down the side of the house, and the garden was very visible to anyone walking in the street if they cared to make it so.

We had just settled down to a nice meal and had poured our second drink when we heard the sound of a car turn into our drive and stop, a car door opened and shut and footsteps approached the gate. Now, the gate was not for security purposes nor was it for privacy. It was effectively an open metal affair, a bit like a five-bar gate, typical of the sort you might find on country walks. This day, through it and over it we saw the approach of Mrs Jenkins. Mrs Jenkins was one of the most senior members of the church. She was a formidable lady, married to another key member of the congregation and office-holder. The church power structure was narrow and at the top was made up of just a few families. Both Mrs and Mr Jenkins were vehemently against alcohol, and Mr Jenkins, especially, against Roman Catholics.

Mr Jenkins was a staunch and loyal member of the Orange Order. He was also proud of the fact that he had signed the protest petition against Margaret Thatcher's 1985 Anglo-Irish Agreement. Unionists had been outraged when the agreement was signed, seeing it as a "sell out," paving the way for a United Ireland. Over 100,000 of them marched to a rally outside City Hall in Belfast in protest against it. It was claimed that 400,000 signed the petition against it. I was told that many did so in blood. Mr Jenkins proudly told me he was one of them.

As Mrs Jenkins came up to the gate and began to open it, in a panic Angela and I moved like the lightning. As if it was

169

a pre-planned and much practised routine, our adrenaline fuelled movements were synchronised with both speed and precision as we neatly secreted the cans of lager, some empty, plus a bottle of wine or two, behind the baby's high chair and turned as one to smile innocently at the approaching visitor. If you have seen the episode of *Only Fools and Horses* in which Rodney wins the art competition for under-15s and the Trotters find themselves on a free holiday in Spain, you will know what I mean. There is that one unforgettable scene, and I apologize to those who have not seen it, where the tour rep. has come to check Rodney's age because he is very obviously much older than 15 (I think he was supposed to be 26 in the programme). If you did see this episode, you will recall the quickest and smoothest sleight of hand, whereby Del Boy turns around with his back obscuring the view of the holiday rep., and removes in one easy, smooth, free-flowing action, the gin and tonic from one of Rodney's hands and the cigarette from the other, before turning back to face the rep. It was a piece of TV magic. One matched by Angela and me in reality as we hid the evidence, much to Seamus and Roisin's astonishment. We did explain to them later that our community was not as relaxed about these things as theirs was, and it was seen that I had a certain position to uphold.

As Angela secreted the remaining evidence from the sight of the fast approaching Mrs Jenkins, I went to meet her to give us a few extra seconds, blocking her view of the table and its contents. By the time she got too close to the table the evidence had vanished. I deliberately kept her away from our guests as I did not want a repeat of the

170

earlier embarrassment for them. I could not be sure how Mrs Jenkins would react. Perhaps I was doing her a disservice, but I could not be sure after the earlier experience with Linda, who was the one we thought least likely to react in such a way. If Linda had responded like this, how might Mrs Jenkins respond? We could not put our guests through that again, or worse. It must have seemed very odd to Mrs Jenkins that I was keeping her at a distance from the table and our guests, and very rude that I did not introduce her. Like many of our congregation Mrs Jenkins would have been very curious as to whom our visitors were. This probably came about from living in a small tight-knit community, where strangers stood out like a sore thumb. The thing I remember most is trying to avoid breathing alcoholic fumes over Mrs Jenkins as she tried to walk a little further towards the table. I held my ground. Mrs Jenkins eyed me suspiciously, I just knew she had identified my fumes as alcohol, but she finally gave in and made her way from the manse, looking back quizzically at me as she went on her way.

A near tragedy in the manse

By this time we were feeling more than a little battered and in the pursuit of a little more privacy we cleared away the BBQ things and made our way back indoors, where we sat at the kitchen table for coffee. The children asked if they could go off and play indoors. We all agreed that it would be safe and we asked Alex, who was about nine or ten, to keep an eye on the younger ones and to call us if there were any problems. Off they went to play. Little did we know there was a near tragedy about to happen.

The children had been gone for about ten minutes when we heard the youngest child of our visitors, Sarah, calling, "Mammy, Mammy."

"Yes dear," said her mum. "I am in here," she called out, expecting her daughter to run down the hall to find her. Sarah was quite safe, after all the front door was locked, she was inside, the house was a child safe area, or so we thought, and Alex was there to keep an eye on things. But things had gone terribly wrong.

The children had explored the upstairs of this large and rambling manse and had gone in and out of the girl's bedrooms. Our son was just a few months old and had his cot in with us, still. The girls had been playing happily and then Sarah, the youngest of daughter of Seamus and Roisin had decided that she wanted to see Mammy. We were a little worried about her walking up and down the stairs and so had fixed the safety gate at the top. This meant that the children were all safe on the upper floor of the manse. The problem was that little Sarah was not happy when she found that it was impossible to get past the safety gate and down the stairs to find Mum.

She, it turned out, was a resourceful little girl. She returned to the top landing and obviously peered down through the gap in the railings of the handrail which surrounded the landing to stop people of all ages falling a considerable distance to the hall floor below. She must have stood there and peered down to the pink-carpeted hall below and from there called to her mum. This was the call we heard from the kitchen at the far end of the hall. She called again. Still there was no sign of Mum. She must have heard Mum's voice, "Yes, dear, I am in here." But Mum was unaware as to where Sarah was. None of us knew. By this time the poor child was desperate to get to her mother and hearing her mother's voice call out from below, she tried to find another way down. After all, the stairs down were blocked by the safety gate. So Sarah started to squeeze her way through the bars of the wooden railings which formed part of the handrail surrounding the top landing, ironically there as a safety precaution.

****

In the kitchen we all froze as we heard a blood curdling scream. Alex had come out from one of the bedrooms to look for little Sarah, her charge. She was terrified to see Sarah squeezing herself halfway through the railings, her little body just able to make it through. This is when Alex screamed.

In the kitchen, after a second's pause, we all rushed to and then through the kitchen door and up the hall. We were just in time to see Sarah crash to the hard floor before our very eyes. She had fallen a long way onto the unforgiving surface, and we were powerless to do anything to help her. Just as Alex had rushed to get to her, Sarah had managed to squeeze her body completely thorough the five inch or so gap in the railings and had plummeted to the floor below.

Roisin, who was a nurse, rushed over to where the limp body of her daughter lay. She checked her vital signs. She screamed for an ambulance. I ran back into the kitchen to where the phone was and dialled 999 and asked for an ambulance. I brought the telephone as close to the door and the hall as the cable would allow me to be as close to the mother and child huddled on the hall floor. The operator was asking me what the trouble was. I tried to explain that the child of about three years of age had had a bad fall of some twelve to fourteen feet onto a very hard surface and was in a very bad way.

As they pressed me for more details and for our address, Roisin shouted, "She is fitting; tell them she is fitting."

I misheard and told the operator that she was "spitting." I thought that she was spitting blood. It did not matter. Thank God that Roisin was a fully trained nurse. She worked on her daughter, doing all she could to restore life into the little one. The shock of the fall had it seemed not only knocked all of the wind from her, but for a moment she lay terribly still. Roisin gave her mouth to mouth and pummelled her chest. Sarah jerked into life and then began the shocking spasmodic jerking of someone who is having a fit, hence the cry of her mother, "She is fitting," not 'spitting'.

We covered the little body with a blanket and waited for the ambulance to arrive. All we could hear was the child's laboured breathing and Roisin's voice above all else. She had done all she could from a practical nursing and medical point of view. It seems she had resuscitated her daughter and calmed her whilst she fitted and until the fit subsided. Now she had only one more thing to do, she prayed. "Holy Mary, Mother of God, blessed is the fruit of your womb, Jesus...Jesus, Mary and Joseph, please don't let her die. Please, God, do not let her die." The prayer went on until the ambulance came. It was there in minutes and took Sarah and her mum to the nearest hospital, Dundonald Hospital just a short drive away.

Seamus and I followed in my car, my old Skoda. He had had more to drink than I, as I had been put off from drinking by the two visits, from Linda and Mrs Jenkins, so I drove. I suspected I was still within the legal limit, but my normal absolute rule about not drinking and driving went out of the

175

window. It was more important for me to get Seamus to the hospital and support him and Roisin in whatever they were to face. I briefly weighed it up and made the decision. I was probably just about ok. We had eaten a large meal and Mrs Jenkins's visit had put me off having another can of lager. It was just as well. I was also sure that any policeman or judge would show me some sympathy under the circumstances. More importantly, I was sure that I would not be a danger to anyone else. I do confess to breaking the speed limit on the way to the hospital, but I was desperate to get there in time. In time for what I did not know, but I just knew that I had to get us there.

When we arrive at A&E, we were ushered through to a side room and there was Roisin and Sarah. By this time the shock had started to show and the little girl was shaking. A doctor was just finishing his examination of her. He made his pronouncement. We expected at least a body and head scan, especially the latter given that she had fitted. But no, we were wrong. The pronouncement was, much to our relief, that there was absolutely nothing wrong with her. She was fine. Sarah lay in her mother's arms, and I think we all shed a tear and shared a prayer of thanks. Sarah was kept in hospital for one night as a precautionary measure, just in case some after effect manifested itself, but next morning she was discharged. She was absolutely fine.

****

Seamus and I had a much slower drive home. Soon after our arrival he gathered up his other daughter and bid us farewell. Angela and I gathered up our children, hugged them and put them to bed, mindful just how fragile life could be and what a lucky escape we had had. There might have been a terrible, terrible tragedy in the manse, but we were very, very lucky. Whether it was the quick thinking reactions of Roisin and her nursing skills, sheer luck or the fervent prayers, or a mixture of all three, I really cannot say. All that mattered then and now is that Sarah was completely unscathed by her ordeal. Thank God.

Free designer clothes and a gift: a wee drop of illegal drink

It was not always easy for us to get hold of alcohol and knowing how disapproving of it many of our congregation were, at least this was the message drummed into us from the start, we were anxious not to cause any offence by flaunting it when we did get it. Although we suspected and had some good and clear evidence that for some, if not many, this was only a public image, and not truly representative of what people did in the privacy of their own homes. We had the feeling that more of the congregation imbibed than would care to admit. We often shared a drink with certain congregants in their own homes, but this was a private thing, like the night in the manse when we celebrated with some senior and key members the end of my fast.

At Christmas one senior member, Brian, always presented us with a large box, delivered under the stealth of night; it was full of goodies for Christmas, the sort he gave out to his clients and always included two or three bottles of spirits. He also gave me some of his suits as he finished with them. He knew how poor we were, he knew my Stipend and he knew the cost of raising a young family. We were of a similar age and build, and he had the most expensive tastes. He was also very fastidious, impeccably dressed and had the income to match his desires. As soon as his clothes became even slightly worn looking, not necessarily worn in the real sense of the term or mine, he would pass them on to the charity shops or during my time there to me. The first time he asked me he was terribly embarrassed by the whole idea, but his spirit of generosity overcame his natural reserve about it. He hinted and hinted then told me what he usually did with the suits he no longer required: it was off to the charity shop with them. Then he commented about how we were of a similar build, and then dropped more hints, until I thanked him for his kind offer. "Yes, I would very much welcome any of the suits which he no longer wanted." I must have been the most expensively dressed minister in the Province at times, beautifully turned out in my latest Dior or Yves St Laurent creation. I must have cut quite a picture, as I picked my way across the farmyards, often through several inches of mud and cow muck, all dressed up in my second-hand designer clothes. All thanks to Brian.

****

Brian truly was a lovely man, for whom I had nothing other than a great deal of respect. A local boy, he had grown up on the small estate which had developed in the village, and he had, we were told by many, "Made good by his own efforts." He was very successful in business and far

179

more outward living, looking and enlightened than most of my congregation, many of whom had experienced only the narrow and inward looking life of the small farmer. This is not referring to their size of course, but to the many who merely farmed a smallholding of a few acres, nothing like the huge empires of the farming corporations or the gentleman farmers back in England. The way of life for the small-time farmers of the Province had not changed for generations, and, indeed, the small areas of land they farmed had been farmed by generations of their ancestors. It was their land, claimed and nurtured by hundreds of years of blood, sweat, tears and toil. Moreover, woe betides anyone who dared to encroach upon it or on their ways. Unfortunately, I did inadvertently, through honesty and naivety not malice, seem to upset a fair few.

From an outsider's point of view it seemed a tough, rigid and uncompromising way of life. There was a sign just along the road from our manse, a sign on the side of the road. Just set back a little, marking the start of the farmer's land. A simple hand-painted sign; with just the post and nothing else surrounded by rusty barbed wire. There was no fence or wire to mark a boundary, just the sign and barbed wire decorated post, not too neat, but a sign which seemed to sum up a certain attitude of mind with a simple, telling and chilling message in red paint:

"TRESPASSERS WILL BE SHOT"

We drove or walked past this sign at least a dozen times a week and each time we honestly felt it was meant; a real warning.

There were other roadside signs around as well. We would often be driving along a nice country road and come across quotes from the Bible:

"REPENT YE OR PERISH"

"THE WAGES OF SIN IS DEATH"

"HOW CAN YE ESCAPE THE DAMNATION OF HELL?"

It was never anything inspiring, uplifting or comforting. It was always a very tough, hardline and uncompromising message: a warning which sounded more like a threat.

****

There was no doubt in our minds that for some there alcohol was a sin (the demon drink) but not for all. A local farmer turned up at the manse one afternoon with a wee present for "His Reverence." It was all whispers, and very cloak-and-dagger, as he kept looking behind him as we spoke at the front door. He asked to come in to present me with a gift, "A wee something for ye."

Odd, I thought, he has nothing in his hands. Then I noticed he had a bit of a bulge under his jacket. It was a typical farmer's jacket: an old suit jacket, which had served well, probably for many years, but still had some service to perform. It was now, inevitably, two sizes too small, splattered with mud or worse, torn in places, adorned with various hairs, his and from various animals, and it smelt of dogs, sheep or cattle. There was usually one of the two front buttons missing, with the one remaining button doing a stoic job in keeping the two sides of the jacket together, or almost. We made our way secretively down the hall and into the kitchen, scene of so much drama during our time at the manse in Moneymore. Still whispering, still furtive, he unbuttoned his jacket, with some relief for at least the button and thread, but probably for him and his comfort as well.

He then produced something wrapped in old brown paper tied up with string. He slowly, almost religiously, unwrapped the parcel. It was rather like a Zen tea ceremony, except rather than serenity covering his unshaven features he was all the while looking suspiciously

182

about him, as if expecting the arrival of the Puritan police. He was especially concerned with the window it seemed to me as I followed his furtive glances from left to right and always back to the window out to the garden. He then revealed the prize. "This is for you, your Reverence. For the cold nights." He added, "Take my advice, go easy with it," and, finally, "I made it myself, but remember this is between ye and me and that's it." He tapped his nose and before I could say a word he turned and shot out of the manse, leaving me looking down at my gift. It was a bottle of a clear(ish), very slightly light yellow, liquid. For a moment I thought he had flipped and brought me a urine sample intended for his GP, after all he had made it himself he said. Then I noticed it was corked and the penny dropped. It was a bottle of homebrew, a bottle of the illegal Potcheen.

Potcheen, also known as Poteen or Poitin in its original Irish form, is a traditional Irish, home distilled, very, very potent alcoholic drink, in other words, "moonshine." It is claimed to be one of the strongest alcoholic drinks in the world, and it was said drinking water the morning after being drunk on it the night before would bring the ethanol still in the body back into solution form and one would get drunk all over again (two for the price of one hangover!). Potcheen was originally distilled from barley or potatoes in a pot, hence its name. For centuries it has been illegal in Ireland, outlawed in 1661.

Aside from the legal issues surrounding Potcheen and taxation, the quality of it I knew could vary hugely.

Historically it was used at weddings and wakes as a cheap form of alcohol, and by some farmers to treat their sick calves. Poorly produced examples were known to contain dangerous amounts of methanol and could blind or kill. And here I was standing holding a bottle of it in the kitchen of the manse, the manse of a church where many of my congregation were vehemently against alcohol of any kind. So, illegal and for many, immoral, sinful even.

I remembered I once had heard talk that a local farmer supplemented his Milk Quota by dabbling in his own homebrew. He was said to brew the best in the area and had to work very hard to avoid the Customs and Excise men and women who were, I was told, on the trail of the "home brewers." It was something I never heard talk of again, and I had forgotten all about it until that moment the penny dropped, standing in the kitchen clutching this bottle. Then, of course, I wondered what should I do with it? What should I do next? Perhaps I should return it to him? After all it was illegally produced and people were sent to prison for this sort of thing. More than this, surely I was implicated somehow? I had just received this illegal gift, although no money had exchanged hands, so there were no taxes or duties to pay, but as I understood it, it was still illegal. I had some while before seen a TV documentary about Potcheen and the constant fight against it by the Customs people on both sides of the border between the Northern Ireland the Republic of Ireland. It was a big issue. And here was I standing in my kitchen, the manse kitchen, knowing how many of my congregation felt about alcohol, holding in my hand a large bottle of this illegal stuff, complete with its much used and battered cork stopper.

On the other hand it was a very kind, if unsolicited and compromising, generous act on his behalf. It sort of meant, I thought, that I was now fully accepted and trusted by the local community, not an easy thing to achieve with all of the people, especially the older farmers who were set in their ways and naturally suspicious of anything or anyone new or different. What should I do? I decided that there was only one thing to do. I could not return it to him as he would be very offended and this would kill any relationship we had built stone dead. I did have the option of handing it in, perhaps without disclosing any details about its source, to the Community Policemen who called by regularly at the manse to converse with me and to share local news and issues. I soon decided this, too, was out of the question. I suspected that for most of the people I was dealing with this would be seen as grassing and that was a dangerous business in Northern Ireland. I simply could have poured it down the sink and thrown away the bottle and wiped out the memory of this gift, but this would have been a terrible waste, and it was such a kind gesture, one of trust. Besides which, I was intrigued as to what all the fuss was about: what was this Potcheen really like? I decided to hide it at the back of a very inaccessible cupboard and over time to drink it. This way I would dispose of the evidence and the problem in the most fitting way. I would drink it and so do justice to his generosity. What else could I do? And so I did.

It was quite an experience. It wasn't so much an unpleasant taste, it did not have much of one, at least a recognizable one, but it was hellishly strong. He was right I had to go very, very carefully with it, indeed. To be honest it was not something I ever wanted to repeat, and I was very glad when I poured the final dregs from the bottle and threw it away.

The pub which opened just once a year

I did not receive any more Potcheen during my time in Northern Ireland, nor did I ask for any. It was much safer, both legally and for my health, to stick to shop bought alcohol. Regarding this, we were always mindful of my congregation's sensibilities, well we tried to be, as we did not want to offend them, so we would avoid buying it, where possible, in any local store where we might be spotted. By local I mean quite a large area as my congregation were widely spread and it often felt like there were many eyes and spies everywhere, and the bush-telegraph, the gossip grapevine, was ever active. This was shown by the far reaching spread of the news of, and the tittle-tattle which followed, the simple differences of opinion I had with key members of the congregation, leading us to leave my ministry to the congregation at Moneymore. The bad news and rumours echoed for miles and for years. Some say even now there is still talk of it and, "What they did to the poor wee English minister." One thing for sure is that country folk do have long memories.

To purchase any alcohol we wanted, and here I do not want it to seem that we were dependent on it or desperate for it, but, at times, we did feel the need for a drink, we would make sure we were as far away from the area as possible, out perhaps on one of the far flung visits to a member of the congregation, for example when delivering the tangerines and bananas on the days following the harvest services. These were our opportunities to stock up.

There were occasionally times when we ran out and craved a drink. Most people will appreciate what it is like when you really fancy a glass of wine or a beer and there is none in the house. The only question then, usually, is, "Is it worth going out to get some?" or "Can anyone be bothered to walk to the corner shop or get the car out and drive a short distance to the nearest supermarket, Off Licence or shop?" For us it was slightly more complicated. For us it was a matter of where might we get a bottle where we were unknown. Sometimes this meant a long drive and it was not practical and so we did without, albeit reluctantly and at times grumpily. If this happened to be a weekday we were sort of ok because we knew we could get out to some place or other and buy some, but on Sundays it was impossible. I again suspect this is a hangover from the good old Calvinistic puritanical mindset, there seemed to be nowhere open on a Sunday to obtain alcohol. During our first summer pastorate we got used to "dry Sundays" as we called them and the impossibility of buying alcohol on the holy day. Off licences were closed and it was just not available outside of pubs. It would not have been the thing, we suspected, for us to have been seen frequenting pubs.

****

188

There was a pub in the village at the time we moved into the manse, but it was of no use to us at all. It was most definitely not an option for us. Not simply because it would have been too close for comfort, and we feared that we would be spotted and the word would have spread like wildfire, but because this pub was a very, very strange affair. It was just along the road from the manse, another small, grey building standing back from the road. It was so nondescript it was easy to pass it by without even knowing it was there. There was certainly no way of knowing it was a pub. There was no sign at all, neither literally or metaphorically. Even today, I do not know what it was called. More than this it was impossible to get to the pub's door. Surrounding and protecting the whole building was a menacing steel and barbed wire fence. The small, rundown building, which obviously still had some remnants of accommodation in it, as well as the pub's bar, and whatever other facilities that were required for the purpose, toilets say, was completely and absolutely inaccessible. It would not have been any use to us and our occasional desire for alcohol, even had we wanted to take a chance that our custom there would not be offensive to, or spotted by, members of the congregation (this meant almost everyone who lived in the village and the estate of grey council houses, the executive homes as they were called).

This, the one pub in the village, was another example of the colourful or as some might say eccentric side of Northern Irish life. It was a pub. I was told it was a pub. But I was unable to get into it, try as I might. And try I did, many times. I should explain more about this fortress of a place,

189

and the owner, so heavily protected that it might easily have been mistaken for a police station, except for the fact that police stations were lively and busy places, with people coming and going all the time. This place, this pub, was desolate. There was no sign of life at all. Yet I was told it was a pub. It was still a legally functioning pub.

****

By the end of our stay in Moneymore this derelict looking fortress of a building had been sold and demolished and a brand new, modern, welcoming and thriving pub had replaced it. We never actually went inside this new pub because of the attitude to alcohol some of the key members of my congregation had. I never actually got inside the old pub either. Nor did I ever get to meet the old man Gilcrest who owned it. Yet, he was a lifelong member of my own congregation.

During our first summer trip to Moneymore I called to see every one of the congregation, diligently and enthusiastically. The one member I could not get in to see was Mr Gilcrest. His address was clear and easy to find. It was just a few minutes stroll away from the manse; an easy visit on paper. I arrived for the first time and was puzzled to find no point of access to what looked like a house or out building over in the far corner of the yard. Everywhere was fenced off. There was no obvious way in or out, certainly

190

not without wire cutters and a team from the SAS. There was more wire here than at Colditz. I peered carefully through the razor and barbed wire, and I could just make out what looked like a door and a dirty and cracked window, but no lights were on. It all looked rather disused, uninhabited and uninhabitable, but there was a metal post box on my side of the protective wire fence. I dropped into it my calling card, the church Communion Card, on it a hastily scrawled message in biro, "Sorry to have missed you, and I hope I get to see you soon."

All the while I was thinking, "Surely, there must have been a mistake. I had been given the wrong information. No one could be living there."

The next time I met with a key member of the congregation I mentioned this to her. "Och, well," she muttered, stroking her chin mysteriously, "I think you had better speak to Bob; he will tell you all about Mr Gilcrest." It all seemed like a rather big mystery. I was eager to get to the bottom of it.

The next day I went to see Bob and asked him about Mr Gilcrest and the pub. It was not easy to coax an answer out of him. I was really intrigued as to what all this secrecy was about. What dark mystery was behind all of this shaking of heads and muttering? I was intent on finding out. I persevered and finally Bob told me. Well, it took some while to prise out of him and piece together the whole story and there was no dreadful secret behind it at all; odd perhaps but there was no dreadful secret.

It turned out that Bob had known Mr Gilcrest all of his life. They had worked together at Harland and Wolff Shipyard, where the Titanic was made, also famous for its two great cranes known as Samson and Delilah. Mr Gilcrest and his family before him had owned and run the pub for decades. It was by all accounts a small room, probably the front parlour, which had been converted into a bar area, with a few seats and nothing much else. But it was a convenient watering hole which had served the drinkers of the village for many a year, perhaps always under the cover of darkness. This was the set up for decades, Bob told me; a sort of private members' club without the extortionate fees required by some smart club in London. Here membership came it seems with birthright; you had to be born in the village, or very nearby, and from an accepted family in the know, so fairly exclusive in that sense. I presume all advertising regarding opening times and closing times, if they existed, were now done by word of mouth. This is the way things had worked for years. Then a terrible experience befell Mr Gilcrest, one which was to change this time honoured pattern for ever.

****

I was always shocked to hear about the past experiences of several elderly members of my congregation who had discovered, sometimes during the day or, more often and much worse, during the night, intruders had broken into their homes. In one case it was three tough thugs, "Taigs from Belfast, if you ask me, Reverend Rowley," who broke in and viciously assaulted the elderly and lone occupant of the house. Mary, then 87, told me of her experience of ten years before, when three men had broken in during the dead of night and tied her to a chair. After knocking her about they left with some cash and jewellery, leaving an old lady so petrified that she had to give up living alone in the house she and her husband had built. Her husband had been a builder and the pair of them literally built the house in which they spent all of their fifty-five years of marriage until her husband's death two years prior to this awful assault. She was proud to tell me how she once had been up on the roof helping her husband put on the tiles. "That was in my younger days, of course, Reverend Rowley," she added, as if I thought that her tiny and frail figure, although housing the most fierce and independent of characters, would still be capable of climbing up onto the roof to lay tiles; although I am sure she would have given it a jolly good go had the need arisen. She was still sprightly and game in spite of her advanced years.

Others told me of similar experiences. Not great numbers of people, but a few years before there had been a spate of this type of cowardly and terrifying crime whereby these thugs came out to the country to find easy pickings amongst the elderly living alone. Several of my congregation had suffered it, but thank goodness it seemed to have died out. I asked Mary how she survived it, although I had no real reason to because she was a wonderful character: seen as cantankerous by many, fiercely loyal to her friends, stubborn and independently spirited to the last. I liked Mary. She was a real character. Not everyone agreed. She replied to my question by shrugging, "You know," she said, "you just have to pick yourself up and get on with things." However, she was not able to go back into the house she and her husband built and found new accommodation with her sister.

****

Mr Gilcrest had suffered the same fate. Believing him to have pots of money secreted away in some secret horde the intruders set about him for hours and gave him a terrible beating. After they finally left with whatever valuables they could find, Mr Gilcrest spent some time in hospital. When he was well enough to leave, he, unlike Mary, did return to his home. But it was to be different. He erected a high barbed and razor wire fence and became a virtual recluse.

The story went that since his ordeal Mr Gilcrest opened up just one night a year, simply I was told to keep his licence going. On that occasion it was said a very small number of his old friends from the past were invited by word of mouth to attend and they would sit and yarn about the old days over a beer or two, or more, and no doubt with some whiskey chasers.

Whenever I walked past the old grey gates and wire fences surrounding Mr Gilcrest's home and pub on our vacation visits, or dropped a visiting card into his mailbox, I always felt sad that this man had been reduced to living a reclusive life, effectively behind bars. The wire and gates which kept him safe had become his prison. It was a terrible shame. I never did get to meet him, as he died during a period when we had returned to England for me to carry on with my studies.

The start of a desperate search for a curry

Recalling the often long searches for an off licence where we would not be known reminded me of a time during Angela's pregnancy when she was carrying our son Andy, who was born at the Royal Victoria Hospital, Belfast. Late one night, probably not far off 11.00pm, just as we were about to go up to bed, Angela suddenly announced that she had a desperate craving for a curry.

Feeling very tired, I tried to persuade her that sleep would soon make it go away and that next day we would buy one, or get the ingredients to make one, and in some way satisfy her craving. This was the first time during any of her three pregnancies that she had craved anything at all. Try as I might I could not persuade her. So, off I set on my labour of love on a cold and wet night. I drove into Belfast and I went round and round, up and down all the major roads leading in and out of the city: Stranmillis Road, City Road, The Antrim Road and so on. It was not like today where we find, at least in England, a rich choice of international cuisine on almost every street corner in many, many places. My current high street provides us with countless eateries of all types: Italian, Thai, Chinese, Indian, and more, and several examples of each, each one offering "eat-in" or "carry-out" or the opportunity to telephone for a home delivery. Not so in Northern Ireland, at least then. We did not know of anywhere we could get an Indian takeaway. I am not suggesting such places did not exist, but there was nothing like the huge choice available here in England today. I imagine that, as with many things in Northern Ireland, it would have been like England fifteen or twenty, or more, years before: a conservative culture, built on traditional family values and still a "church-going" and "God-fearing" people, at least for the most part. For many then the idea of a curry was quite foreign.

****

And so it was that I drove around and around. I recalled seeing a takeaway up on the Castlereagh Road, but when I got there it was closed. It looked permanently closed rather than simply closed for the night.

I pulled over to the side of the road and pondered on what I was going to do next? It was now well past midnight, and I was getting nowhere, except more and more frustrated and tired. Yet, I dare not return without the desired vegetable curry, two naan breads and the most desired of all: a pot of mango chutney. Angela had now been waiting for over an hour back in the manse craving, increasingly desperate I was sure and probably salivating. I could not in all good conscience stop at a telephone box to ring home to tell her of my progress, or more accurately the lack of progress, and that I was aborting my mission and coming home. I could not disappoint her, not yet. I would not give up that easily, even though it was looking increasingly unlikely that I would succeed.

There was not much traffic at that time of night. Many people avoided travelling into Belfast at the best of times if they could, for obvious reasons: the risk of a shooting, being caught up in an attack somehow or somewhere, the unpredictability of the bombs and bomb scares and at very least the disruption they caused. Some simply went in for work and got out and home as soon as they could. Some avoided it at all costs. Some would not go there and "that was that."

Here was I sitting alone in a car with English number plates in the middle of Belfast City, short haired and slim (I have already mentioned the issue about the possibility of being mistaken for an off duty soldier) looking for a takeaway curry house, pondering my next move.

****

Then I saw them ahead. A police and Army patrol. Coming towards me, but way ahead further up the road. The three or four armour plated trucks slowed to a halt, blocking half of the road and a number of policemen and soldiers poured out of the vehicles. Some spread out forming a protective security cordon around the impromptu checkpoint which had now been established. Several soldiers were in their customary battle ready position, with gun sights to eyes, scanning the area for potential danger, ready to open fire at the first sign of an attack.

This was a stroke of good fortune for me. I am still not sure who they were hoping to get at that time of night. There were barely any cars on the road. I drove towards the blockade and pulled to a halt as instructed by the lead policeman who had flagged me down with his torch, signalling ever more slowly in an up and down motion. It was quite clear that he wanted me to stop. I wound down my window.

The policeman saw my clerical collar. "On your way, Reverend; I am sorry to have stopped you, Sir." This was not uncommon. He probably thought that I was heading to the hospital up on the Falls or to a death house. Why else would I be out at this time of night?

****

I often wondered why a terrorist did not get a clerical collar, or even make his own from a piece cut out from an empty washing-up liquid container, to get through these regular road blocks. I once created a spare insert in this way when mine went missing and it worked just as well as the real thing. It only mimicked the small type of collar, the little bit of white which showed at the front only, not the full blown and deep type of collar which circumvented the whole neck. The latter was the more visible and impressive and showed everyone exactly who you were.

I was certain that some clerics wore this badge of office for the effect it had. One of my colleagues was never seen out of his collar. He even mowed his lawn in it. I would not have believed it, but I saw it for myself. I often wondered if he wore it in the bath or in bed, and if the day would come when he would have to have it surgically removed. Sadly, this individual seemed to bask in the power it gave him in his own community, the community he had been born into and grown up in. He had worked at the local factory like most of his peers; the only difference was that late in life he had decided to become a minister and now he and his collar were inseparable. It most certainly did set him apart and gave him a certain power he otherwise would not have had. Now he was someone, someone important!

The collar most certainly brought a degree of power in that society. I was more often than not waved through the police and Army checks when wearing mine, and this was a great help if the queue was lengthy, especially on the way into the airport where checks were always more intensive.

So, I was always surprised that terrorists did not try it on in the hope that they would be waved through the checkpoint with ease. I was more often than not. Mind you, I was told by someone in the know that by the time a driver had slowed down and come to a halt the car registration details had been scanned and checked and confirmed. I also suspected that most of the time these random checks had a specific target in mind, a bit like the similar, but illegal, roadblock set up on the mountain road encountered by Margaret and Bill and their friends from England.

****

The night I was out in Belfast desperately searching for a curry the policeman was happy to wave me through the checkpoint with a smile. This was not the case on one occasion for a friend and colleague of mine.

A fake clerical collar and the search for a curry goes on

A sign that the security forces were not gullible when it came to dealing with the clerical collar was clear from an experience of a minister I knew. He told me how he had come up with a neat ploy to enable him to go about much of his day without the trappings of his office and be able to change at the drop of a hat, a bit like a superhero emerging from a telephone box, only here there was no need for a telephone box and a minister appeared. My ministerial colleague and friend Simon was happy to go into town shopping with his wife, and wear "civilian" clothing. Should the need arise for him to visit a hospital or congregant later on, rather than going home to change he would put on a black shirt he kept in his car. He would then slip into the collar a homemade insert along the lines of my washing-up liquid container mentioned above. This worked really well, that is until the day he was flagged by an Army roadblock.

Perhaps he was just unlucky that day. His luck seems to have been out because there was not a native born member of the Royal Ulster Constabulary, a policeman to you and me, present who might have been a little more aware and understanding of the sometimes eccentric ways of some of the local clerics. Indeed, a Belfast bobby would probably have recognized my friend, passed a friendly moment of chat with him and then waved him on his way smiling. This did not happen on this occasion.

The soldier, a young Englishman, perhaps on his first tour of duty in the Province, was quite obviously not from these parts. He asked my friend who he was and for some ID, at the same time he seemed to notice that my friend's white clerical collar strip was slipping out of his ordinary, non-clerical, black shirt collar. The more my friend felt and fumbled around on his person, from pocket to pocket and back again, searching for some form of ID, the more dishevelled his clothing became, and the more the white strip slipped out of his collar. It soon became obvious that my friend was wearing two shirts and the black shirt and clerical collar had been put on over his normal clothes. It must have looked like a very poor attempt at a disguise; a very bad effort to superimpose the persona of a cleric who would have an air of innocence about him and give a readymade passport into all sorts of places. On realizing that he had no ID, Simon explained his plight and apologized. The soldier called over a colleague.

Simon was getting a little hot under the collar himself by then. Everyone carried ID in Northern Ireland for this very reason. He realized how it must be looking. Then, and why he did this under the circumstances he said he really did not know, but it was a stupid and dangerous thing to do given the context, Simon started to open the glove compartment of the car, just in case he had left his Driver's Licence in there, or by chance would find some other papers to help support his claim as to who he was and where he lived.

The soldier screamed out and ordered him to "STOP." "F***ING WELL STOP NOW." "STOP OR I WILL BLOW YOUR F***ING HEAD OFF." There was a flurry of activity, and other colleagues arrived. Simon was roughly pulled out of the car, held spread-eagled against the car and searched. They thought they had caught a "live one." They were taking absolutely no chances at all. And who could blame them? Often these road blocks were the target for terrorist activities. They could be shot at, or have petrol bombs thrown at them, hence the red-alert posturing of these patrols and convoys most of the time.

****

It was not unusual when driving to follow behind an Army patrol, a convoy of four or five armoured vehicles, and face the disconcerting sight of the wrong end of an automatic weapon, held in firing position at the soldier's shoulder, with the sight at his eye as he surveyed around for possible threats, ready for an instant response. It did not make for a happy or relaxing journey if you spent 15 minutes travelling slowly behind the convoy, staring up the barrel of a gun. I often wondered what if the soldier was stressed or trigger happy? Anything was possible under such intense conditions. What would happen if a nearby car backfired at the wrong moment, or, as I once said to Angela as we followed yet another convoy and were staring down another barrel, what would happen if he sneezed? She did not reply, but just slapped my leg, hard. The price I paid for an attempt, a poor and ill-timed effort, to make light of a tense situation. It was always a welcome sight to see the convoy turn off onto another road, or to know that our turning to take us in a different direction was just a hundred yards and a few seconds ahead.

I always felt for the young soldiers and police who had to man these roadblocks and checkpoints. They knew they faced all sorts of terrible possibilities, petrol bombs thrown under the vehicles, gun attacks from nearby or from a passing car, vehicles packed with explosives and driven straight at them. And then there was the most bizarre activity of all given the intense and dangerous context, "joy riders." It was an increasing phenomenon: young, unemployed youths, stealing cars, especially in West Belfast, I was told, and driving straight at and through these checkpoints which were protected with heavily armed soldiers and police, who were on red-alert for attacks from terrorists.

****

An attack which took place on the permanent checkpoint on the Belfast-Dublin Road at South Armagh is a prime example of what the soldiers and police who manned these points across the Province might expect at any time.

205

I was told that four IRA volunteers held a family hostage late one night and stole their mechanical excavator. Others stole a van and loaded it with hundreds of pounds of explosives. The van was equipped with wheels to make it run along railway tracks, for the Belfast to Dublin railway line crossed the main road where the checkpoint was. The excavator lifted the van onto the tracks, it was then driven to a hill some 800 metres north, where a long wire attached to a triggering device was added to the van. Meanwhile, IRA support teams set up roadblocks in order to prevent civilians from approaching the area.

Around 2.00am the vehicle was clamped into first gear and directed at the checkpoint. A British patrol heard the noise of a "train" heading towards the checkpoint, which was immediately alerted.

At 2.05am the bomb went off, claiming the life of one soldier at the checkpoint. It could easily have been several more.

****

How difficult it must have been for those manning the checkpoints to decide in a split second if the car racing towards them was a terrorist attack and packed with explosives or carrying a gunman, or an "innocent" joy rider. There were, it goes without saying, a number of terrible incidents in which, inevitably, young lives were tragically and unnecessarily lost. What a terrible waste. How strange is the term 'joy riding'?

The effects on the community of such anti-social behaviour were profound. This was when it was said the people were better "protected" by the paramilitaries, who dispensed their own often brutal method of punishment for such anti-social behaviour such as child abuse, drug peddling and joy riding and the like. Some factions of the community trusted their own terrorist godfathers more than they did the police. This was said to be especially true of the non-Protestant community who feared the security forces were too heavily connected to the Protestant community to deal with them fairly.

****

Given all of the tensions and the ever present possibility of attacks, it was no wonder that my friend Simon was given rather a rough time. He had no ID and seemed to be masquerading as a minister or priest. And these were dangerous times. Times when people from both sides of the sectarian divide, as well as from the police force and the Army, were being killed or maimed. It is no wonder suspicions were roused. My friend was roughly manhandled, bundled into the back of one of the vehicles and taken to a nearby police station.

I have already noted that the police stations were fortresses. You could not just pop in the front door and queue at the front desk to show your car insurance document, complain about a neighbour or ask directions as you might elsewhere in the world. In Northern Ireland at the time the police stations were all encased in huge, grey, steel security fencing, with copious amounts of razor wire and huge gates. It was all floodlit at night, brighter than daylight. There was often an entry point which one could approach. A sort of lookout tower, with a letter box shaped communication slot. Too small to put a bomb through, one could call through to the watchmen inside what your business was and why you wanted entry. They were fortresses, also on red-alert, having been the targets of many attacks. It was to the nearest police station Simon was taken, and there he had the task of explaining what he was doing wearing two outfits at the same time, with the unconvincing clerical garb on top. He was there for some hours, until another cleric, known to one of the policemen was brought in to identify him and corroborate exactly who he was. Then he was released, none the worse for his experience. I am sure the police and the soldiers had a good laugh about it all after he left and remembered for a long time the evening they arrested a minister on the suspicion of terrorism.

Simon never again used a small piece of washing up liquid bottle and a black shirt in place of his official clerical garb.

****

On the night I was desperately seeking a curry for my pregnant wife, the policeman waved me on my way with a smile. I did not recognize him, but it was possible he knew me. He looked surprised as I stopped, wound down my window and asked for his help. He was grinning from ear to ear as I explained what I was doing out on the dark streets of Belfast at this very later hour. He did not know of an Indian takeaway himself, "I cannot stand the stuff, Sir," he said, "but I know who will know." He kindly radioed one of his colleagues and was soon able to give me directions to take me to the most likely source to satisfy my wife's craving: a curry house just ten minutes way up on the Lisburn Road. I thanked him for his kindness and set off.

I arrived just as the manager was closing up. He was just turning around the "OPEN" sign in the window to show "CLOSED." I parked up outside and raced to the door. He saw the collar and opened the door. Thank goodness I was wearing it. When I explained I was on a mission of mercy for my pregnant wife the manager was absolutely brilliant. He quickly sorted out the food I requested, threw in some extras, after all he said, it was all going to waste tomorrow, and I left, triumphant, clutching my takeaway bag, my mission accomplished.

****

I got home about 12.45am or so. The house was quiet. Angela was upstairs in bed. I locked up and rushed up to her. "I have got it," I shouted, forgetting the children were asleep. I added, "It has been a nightmare, but I have got it." "Do you want it up here or downstairs?"

Angela looked up at me, smiled and sleepily said. "Where have you been? I am sorry it took you so long. It's ok. After you left I had a cup of tea and the feeling went. The craving's gone."

I was stunned. "Just have a little," I said, almost pleading.

"I couldn't," she replied. "In fact the very thought of it now makes me feel quite sick."

Ironically, Angela never had a craving for curry during her other two pregnancies, nor did she again whilst carrying Andy.

It was only that once, just the once, very late on that very dark and very cold night, and it was very short lived.

The curry? The curry ended up in the bin.

Back in the manse: a meeting twice over, charity dispensed and vital money abruptly taken away

Life in ministry continued on relentlessly, following its usual pattern of services and visiting. Life in the manse followed its usual pattern, too. Family life went on as normal, as best it could. It was inevitably affected by the demands ministry placed on me and the many intrusions into the manse.

Some church meetings took place in my study, not just meeting up with the would-be bride and groom in preparation for their wedding arrangements or seeing individuals about all sorts of issues, but more formal and larger gatherings. I did have a very large study. It was very impressive: the larger of the two front rooms, just off the large hall as you came in from the front door. This was a strategic move by us when we arrived and planned out which room would be which and who would have which bedroom and so on. Our reasoning was that the smaller of the two front rooms was large enough to be a family room, with the TV, and it had a working fireplace still, and so the possibility of a roaring fire. We decided that the larger of the two front rooms would make an ideal study to house my ever growing collection of books. My collection stood at over 1500 by this time, collected up from purchases for the various academic courses I had done, as well as second-hand bookshops and legacies to me from various elderly minister friends of mine who either retired or died, or retired and then died. This larger room would also serve as a meeting place for the many visitors we knew would find their way to the manse: the community policemen, complete with bullet-proof vests, flak-jackets, handguns and automatic rifles, who called by for a cup of tea and a chat as they patrolled the village; complete strangers who wanted something from me or the church and many, many members of the congregation, most of whose ancestors had paid into the fund which built the church or had actually had a hands on role in its erection, cutting the bricks and mixing mortar and the like.

****

I was the Honorary Secretary to two charitable funds at the time as both of these positions went with the ministry of Moneymore Church. The money to set up these funds had come from the legacies of two very wealthy families connected with the church: the Potters, whose generosity gave birth to the Potter Benevolent Fund, and the Bodell-Maginty family, whose generosity gave rise to the unsurprisingly named Bodell-Maginty Fund. It was my role as secretary to send out the twice-yearly grant application forms to the benefactors. Much of the detail which follows is a mere hazy memory, but as I recall claimants were restricted to spinsters and widows of a certain age, 60, and over, I think, who were judged to be of good Christian character (!) and living within a certain local boundary. The beneficiaries had to apply each time for their grants and forms were sent out by me, completed by the recipient and returned to me. This all by hand and pen, as there was no computer or database to help then.

There were about 150 beneficiaries of each fund, and this process occurred twice a year. The problem was the grants were restricted by some clause in the original deeds of the charities and try as we might we could not get them changed. In effect the cheques, all drawn up by hand, and very gratefully received by the spinsters and widows of Moneymore and area, were tiny, about £10 a time, tiny that was in comparison to the trusts' funds which in both cases ran into hundreds of thousands of pounds. Following the original legacies many decades before, in loving memory of these two grand and respected families, the money had been well and wisely invested in stocks and shares and now both funds were thriving. The problem was they kept growing as the total amount of grants given out over the year proved to be just a tiny percentage of the income from the fund's investments and the excess was reinvested. Both funds were overflowing with money. It was a frustrating situation, one which probably still exists to this day.

As secretary to the funds, I gave formal notice to the committee members of the meetings to approve the drawing up and distribution of the cheques to existing members and to assess new claims for membership. The meetings for both funds took place on the same evening, twice a year, and, as I recall, there was also an Annual General Meeting as well, again one for each fund, held on the same evening. It was all very formal, as were most things in the church there in Moneymore.

The dozen or so committee members would meet in my study to listen to the treasurer's report about how well the fund had done in the past six months, and occasionally to hear that a certain Miss X's cheque had been sent back from the bank because she had forgotten to cash it within the six month limit whilst it was still "live," or that she had died before she had cashed it. My report would usually involve applications from would-be beneficiaries upon whom we had to vote. Then we would bring the meeting to a close formally, just as it had been opened, with prayer, with all of this carefully recorded. Then the one or two committee members who sat only on the first committee would depart to make their way home, and we would be joined by one or two who sat only on the second committee and we would begin all over again. The same formal process was observed each time. A very formal welcome and an opening prayer, remember we had just spent the past hour or so in the company of pretty much the same group of men. It was all men of course as this was "responsible work," as I was once told when I asked why there were no ladies on either committee!

And then off we would go again. Everything was repeated in much the same detail. The same people would inevitably be applying for both funds, but we had to read through, discuss in detail and approve each one again. If a cheque for Miss X had been returned "un-cashed" at the first meeting it was almost certain that another in her name from the other fund would be returned at the second meeting. Yet, still we had to go over all the detail. All of which was carefully recorded in the minutes.

Almost without exception all of the beneficiaries received benefit from both funds: two cheques for each person twice a year, each one requiring a formal application, countersigned by me.   After the second meeting was concluded with yet another prayer, I, for the second time that evening, declared very formally that "This meeting is now closed." This too was recorded in the minutes, complete with the time it was said. Angela then wheeled in the hostess trolley piled high with the sandwiches she had just spent the evening making and cakes, biscuits and tea. The chat often went on long into the night.

****

At least I was not expected to deliver by hand all of the cheques as I had feared when I first heard of this additional role which accompanied my ministry in Moneymore. Those beneficiaries who had moved I recall were allowed to retain their benefits, and I was allowed to post off the cheques to those who lived at a distance. I still had to deliver quite a few by hand.

215

Although the grants were comparatively miserly compared to the great wealth of both funds, it was a nice scheme to be involved in, even if I so badly wanted to send a much greater sum to each of the beneficiaries. The really helpful thing for me trying to provide for my family on a very low income was that the Honorary Secretary, in this case me, received an allowance for his work. This came to a few hundred pounds it total from both funds. For us it was a life saver. It really did mean the difference of financial survival or not. This made it even more of a shock, and even more painful, when one of my colleagues, a senior minister who had some strong connections with and obvious influence over members of both committees made sure that I was not able to carry on with my role as secretary to the funds when my ministry in Moneymore was coming to an end. He knew how dependent we were on that extra money; he knew that we had three children and the youngest was a mere two years old; yet he was quoted as saying, "We will starve him out." Even after studying theology for five years prior to becoming a minister, I can never quite recall the exact text from the Bible to support this attitude.

The beginning of a particularly eventful evening in the manse: a tale of infidelity

So, life in the manse rolled on with a predictable pattern; that was until the unpredictable broke in to disturb it, which, come to think of it was pretty often. There was always something happening in the manse. One very strange evening which stands out as particularly memorable, unfolded on a dark winter's night. I had been out all day visiting and had arrived home very tired, looking forward to seeing the family and having a bit of a rest in front of the television, a rare treat. How wrong I was.

The early part of the evening was fairly typical. We ate in the kitchen, enjoying the heat of the oven, and were in the process of deciding what to watch on TV when the telephone rang. I answered it and it was a very distressed Mrs Boggs, sobbing her heart out down the 'phone. Mrs Boggs explained to me that she had just been given some dreadful news and asked if she could she come and see me at once. "Of course," I said, "come around straight away." I noticed Angela pull a face at me from out of the corner of my eye, but said nothing. After all it was only 6.30pm and there was still time for a nice ordinary evening in front of the coal fire and the TV in the front room. More than this, it did sound something of great urgency, not like the time I took a telephone call asking me to visit someone, no one very young, old, ill or vulnerable, who had (how shall I say it without being overtly lavatorial in my description?) a bad tummy upset. What on earth they thought I could do about it defied me then and defies me even to this day. That was one call I was too busy to make. I was otherwise engaged, so to speak.

Back in the manse this particular evening, I sank down into the armchair in front of the fire until Mrs Boggs arrived. This was within ten minutes of me putting down the receiver in the kitchen. I prised my way out of the comfy chair and went to the front door to let her in. She looked dreadful. She was obviously in a state of shock. I gently led her into the other front room, the study, and sat her down. She was visibly shaking as she began to tell me of her woes, stopping only to sob. Poor Mrs Boggs was almost literally sobbing her heart out. This was serious.

I was always deeply touched at such times when individuals would come and share with me on a very deep and personal level. It might be to get something off their chest and more than once I was told, "I have never told anyone else this," not even wife or husband, indeed not one living soul. It was a great privilege and a responsibility, and I hoped that by unburdening to me in this way the person would feel "lighter" and somehow freed from a heavy burden or chains from the past. It might be someone struggling to come to terms with a serious illness, bereavement, or some other major challenge on the journey of life. For me this was what ministry was all about, not delivering the endless Communion Cards or the

218

tangerines and bananas to an address many miles away after the harvest services. This was real. It was not that I thought I had the answers to people's problems or a magic formula to dispense, but simply in the sharing of and with support over time, more often than not, comfort, understanding or acceptance was found.

On this occasion, and I would not dream of going into any more detail, poor Mrs Boggs had been told by her husband of many years, just before she had telephoned me, that he had been having an affair with a much younger women. Poor Mrs Boggs' world fell apart.

So we sat and shared. It was a long sharing. Reviewing her life with the man she thought was devoted to her; re-visiting memories of long ago and pondering her future; all interspersed with long periods of silence or sobbing.

****

Mrs Boggs had been in with me for about an hour-and - a-half or so when I heard another knock on the door, then after a long pause the sound of the door being opened and the muffled sound of voices. When I say voices it was only one voice really, Angela's. I could just about make out Angela's voice as I continued to give Mrs Boggs my full, well almost full, attention as she continued to share and sob. But I could not make out the other voice. Well it wasn't a voice really, more a sound, the sound of someone gasping for breath. What on earth was it, I thought, still fighting to give Mrs Boggs my full attention?

Then it came. A piercing scream broke into my forced attentiveness to Mrs Boggs. The moment was shattered. It was Alex. A scream, then a shout, "Mum, Dad, come quick."

****

I found out a little later that the other voice or sound I heard at the door whilst I was intently engaged with Mrs Boggs was in fact heavy breathing coming from an elderly man, Mr Robertson, a very honest and devout member of the congregation, a real character, a farmer, who had arrived at the manse for some purpose long since forgotten. He was unable to speak to Angela because he was doubled up, clasping his chest, unable to breathe, supporting himself on the pillar of the porch. Any attempt he made at talking came out in the most eerie sound, shrouded by the heavy breathing and his laboured struggle for breath, which Angela later said reminded her of the death-rattle she had once heard many years ago when she was present at the death of her elderly aunt. Here stood this poor old man, tears from his efforts to talk and, possibly, breathe, streaming down his face. When I say stood, it is an exaggeration, if Angela's later description was accurate. Here on the doorstep of the manse, he held on to the porch as if he was holding out against the call of death itself, refusing to let go. Angela saw him clutching the doorframe and the state of him, and quite naturally assumed he was having a heart attack. Her re-telling of the events painted quite a picture. It still does.

* * * * * * *

Whilst I was in the front room with a desperate and distraught Mrs Boggs, Angela had been on the telephone in the kitchen, standing at the very same spot where I had been talking to Mr Jones a couple of years before during our first summer pastorate in Northern Ireland, the time when Dorothy had almost caught me naked as my tiny hand towel, the only protection I had to spare my blushes, and to save Dorothy's, fell to the tiled floor. Angela had been on the phone to another elderly congregant who was in need, we cannot now recall who it was or the need, Angela was patiently explaining that Reverend Rowley had someone with him at that moment, and, "Yes he would ring back or pop round as soon as he had a moment." Getting this message across was proving to be quite a task as the lady was quite deaf, deaf but quite insistent that she wanted to "speak to Reverend Rowley."

At that moment came the knock on the front door. Angela, perhaps in order to get a brief respite from shouting down the phone that Reverend Rowley had someone with him at the moment, but, "Yes, he would ring back when he

221

was free," and, "Yes, he would pop round as soon as he could," left the telephone off the hook, and, with the lady's voice still asking to speak to Reverend Rowley, made her way of escape, down the hall towards the front door, the same route but in reverse Dorothy had taken as she had let herself into the manse a couple of years before.

This time it was Angela leaving the kitchen. She reached the front door and opened it to find Mr Robertson, doubled up, with tears streaming down his face, and thought he was having a heart attack. She stood back as he looked up at her and tried unsuccessfully to speak.

She had just started to call for me. Then it came. A piercing scream which broke into my focus on Mrs Boggs, the moment was gone. It was Alex. First the scream, then a shout, "Mum, Dad, come quick. Andy has drunk the Tipp-Ex."

A suspected heart attack and a drink of Tipp-Ex correction fluid

The old saying tells us "It never rains but it pours." This was never more relevant than on this particular evening in the manse, or at least it seems to us. We had Mrs Boggs whose world had just collapsed in the front room; we had the elderly lady on the telephone still demanding to "speak to the Reverend Rowley," and now we had Mr Robertson on the front door step clutching his chest with one hand and the porch for support with the other. Just as Angela reached out to support him before he fell over, and began to call for me, Alex's piercing scream rang out followed by her shout, "Mum, Dad, come quick. Andy has just drunk the Tipp-Ex."

Roused by the scream, I leapt from my chair and shot out of the front room almost colliding with Angela who had turned from Mr Robertson, who was still clutching at his chest and the frame of the porch, whilst struggling to take even the smallest amount of breath. We both turned to look up the stairs, in the general direction of the scream and the shout. We saw Alex standing on the first landing looking terribly frightened. She was clutching Andy's hand. Andy stood beaming at us, as if wondering what all the fuss and excitement was about. It was not only a broad smile which decorated his face, but all around his mouth was a white substance, a fluid, paint like, which already was beginning to dry and flake. It was then we began to make sense of

Alex's words, shouted out in panic following her scream, "Mum, Dad, come quick. Andy has just drunk the Tipp-Ex." And he had. About half a bottle of correction fluid, we later calculated.

We were caught in a number of ways, but this was serious, or potentially so. Angela rushed up the stairs to grab hold of Andy screaming to me that Mr Robertson was on the doorstep having a heart attack. Mrs Boggs who by now, drained of all tears, had managed to compose herself, peered around the door of the front room and politely asked if there was anything she could do to help. I asked her to help me with Mr Robertson and between us, with the support of the wall, we managed to get him sat down in an armchair in the front room. I rushed out shouting that I would telephone for an ambulance. I wasn't sure if I would need one or two.

I ran to the kitchen where Angela had taken Andy. Alex stood there looking petrified. This was not long after the episode of Sarah falling through the stair railings. This was very fresh in all of our minds. Poor Alex must have thought, "Oh no, here we go again."

I made a leap for the telephone and as I raised it to my ear I could hear the voice still insisting indignantly, "I only wanted to speak to the Reverend Rowley, that is all." Having no idea as to who was on the other end of the line, I blurted out that I would ring back as soon as I could, but I had to ring for an ambulance as we had a crisis in the manse. I did not try to explain that we needed two, perhaps. I slammed down the phone.

In my panic, I slammed it down so hard that it did not make a proper connection, and I could not at first get a dial tone. This made me bang it down even harder. All I wanted to do was to dial 999. Then Angela's voice cut through my thoughts. I was thinking about our son, our lovely, precious, two year old son; what was happening to his insides. What could we do to minimize any harm which might be taking place inside him second by second, minute by minute? It is amazing how many thoughts can flood through your mind in a very short space of time. I also thought what would the hospital authorities think, with us calling them out for another child in trouble, at the same address? It is strange what thoughts pass through our minds at certain times.

Angela's voice cut through my thoughts. Unknown to me, all the while I had been helping Mr Robertson into the front room, with the assistance of Mrs Boggs and the wall, Angela had been asking questions of Alex and piecing together exactly what had happened. The children and one or two school friends had been playing safely in one or other of the bedrooms when Andy, now bored, had tottered off on his own to explore. He had discovered in one of the girl's school satchel a small white container of Tipp-Ex correction fluid. He must have been very intrigued, at least intrigued enough to play around with the cap and persevered until it came off. He them proceeded to drink it. At some point, perhaps satisfied with his success, he wandered back towards the bedroom, his face covered in white. Alex said he appeared at the bedroom door and looked very pleased with himself, until she screamed and rushed towards him. At this he dropped the Tipp-Ex

225

container, then turned and made for the stairs. Alex caught up with him on the landing. It was then she shouted out for Angela and me.

****

By the time I was trying to telephone for an ambulance, Alex had retrieved the discarded bottle from the bedroom, brought it to Angela who was scrutinizing it for the vital details. Breathing a sigh of relief she discovered it was non-toxic. I am not even sure that we knew such a thing was an option at that time. Even now we have only faded memories of an alternative to the original becoming available because of some sort of substance abuse issue, with some schools banning its use completely.

Angela called over to me not to ring for an ambulance as it seemed everything was ok. We talked over the evidence on the bottle and the fact that Andy seemed as right as rain, but decided on taking some precautionary measures just to be on the safe side. We rang the hospital, A&E, and asked for their advice. After reading out the long and at times almost unpronounceable list of contents on the back of the bottle, and after an even longer wait, the A&E nurse returned to the phone to tell us that they were not at all concerned, but it might be better to bring him in to take a look. So off we set. Mrs Boggs said she would look after the manse, and we bundled the children into our old Skoda and set off for the hospital which was a short distance away, the same hospital where so recently Sarah was taken by ambulance after falling through the railings in the manse hall and to where Seamus and I sped in hot pursuit and in fear for her life.

After a short check as a precaution to determine that Andy was absolutely fine (there was nothing dangerous in the ingredients, even for a two year old) we returned home. There we found Mrs Boggs and Mr Robertson talking away, catching up on the local gossip and farming news.

Mr Robertson had not in fact been having a heart attack at all. He was experiencing awful problems breathing in the cold, damp weather. It was not his heart that was causing his distress, it was his lungs. He had a bad and chronic chest complaint. He had rushed up the hill too quickly and the cold air had hit him badly. By the time he reached the manse he was barely able to breathe or stand. But it was not a heart attack. He soon recovered sitting down in the comfortable armchair in the warmth of the front room of the manse, with a nice cup of tea in his hand, made by Mrs Boggs whilst we were at the hospital.

****

Thank God, Andy was completely unharmed by the experience. He recalls none of it, of course, and any insights or faint memories he has of it have come from hearing us repeat the story many times. The story could so easily have had a tragic ending if the liquid he drank had been of the toxic variety. It does not bear thinking about.

Whenever I tell this story, as I have done many times over the years, I like to leave it on a lighter note. I always conclude by saying that every cloud has a silver lining and that I am proud that Andy has never made a spelling mistake since.

Special Services: a newborn lamb in church and giving them the "whole bloody bucketful"

Breaking up the regular, weekly, "bread and butter" Sunday services were the special services: Mothering Sunday, Palm and Easter Sundays, Harvest, which I have mentioned, Christmas Day and the twice-yearly Communion Services and so on. In order to boost attendance on Sundays, I introduced some new special services, such as ones with visiting speakers telling us of the work of UNICEF, for example, and a monthly Children's service, where all the children of Sunday School were encouraged to join us for the whole service and not just the first part of it to leave after the first hymn as usual. The sermon time was given over to a long children's story with a spiritual or moral message.

I still recall the look on the children's faces, some as young as three or four, during one such service as they were invited to come to the front of the church to bottle feed by hand a newborn lamb. That one took some work to get the timing right, I can tell you. The children knew nothing about it at all; they simply gathered for the usual monthly service where they would stay in church with their parents. The theme was about Jesus the shepherd and at the appropriate moment the children were told to expect a visitor. One tiny boy called out and asked if it was going to be Santa. His eyes bulged as did the rest of the congregation's, both young and old, when they saw the door of the church open and in came a local farmer, a member of the congregation who had been up all night lambing. He had promised, if possible, to bring to the church his most recently born lamb. And he did. He brought it up to the front of the church, to the Communion Table, and stood there beaming, as proud as punch, jacket tied together around his waste with string, straight from all night in the field lambing, muddy boots on the pristine carpet and all. It was magical.

The children delighted in coming up to the front to feed the lamb warm milk from a baby's bottle. I am not sure that they remembered anything of the spiritual message, but they sure enjoyed the experience of seeing the tiny lamb being carried into church, taking it in turns to hold the bottle, whist the lamb suckled on it, oblivious to everything that was going on around it. Neither was I too sure as to exactly what the future had in store for it one Sunday soon, but it did not take too much of an imagination to work it out. I dare not ask, but it was unlikely it was bred to be a pet. I remember thinking, as a strict vegetarian, the idea of "gentle Jesus, meek and mild" did not really enter into it.

This was not the only time we had an animal in church, but next time the animal in question was not only too shy or stubborn to come alone, it insisted two friends would have to come as well; and it disgraced itself more than once on the church carpet.

****

Whilst the ordinary services all followed the typical non-conformist pattern of the "hymn sandwich," with four hymns providing the framework for the service, separated by the filling of various sorts, including two readings, one from the Old Testament and one from the New, prayers, musical offerings from the organist and choir (which practised the four hymns and musical offerings religiously on a Thursday evening of each week from 8.00pm until 9.00pm without fail) and, if possible, a soloist. And the crowning glory, the sermon.

The sermon was in theory the climax of the service. The preached word was considered to be the way of accessing spiritual manna. Not in this tradition was there a priestly caste which would dispense or withhold blessings, hear confessions and then give forgiveness. This church was in the Protestant tradition. Each believer was encouraged to develop his or her own faith, and part of this process was to listen to the word of God read (the two readings) and interpreted and pronounced on in the sermon. My own religious position was far less conservative than we encountered in the Province, a very left wing, liberal theologically, but boy-oh-boy, was I enthusiastic. I took my role very seriously and the congregation got their money's worth, whether they wanted it or not.

I was not talking down to anyone and never claimed to have the answers to life's mysteries, but I took seriously the charge laid upon me at my Ordination to assist the education of the flock in spiritual matters and I did try. Did I try. I tried to make my sermons rich, varied, informative and interesting. I would never restrict the content to biblical themes. I would always take up contemporary issues and so on, and my only goal was to stimulate thinking and discussion. But, did my poor congregation suffer. I was very keen you see, very new, very keen and very enthusiastic. The generally accepted rule is that the ideal sermon is a short one, which leaves "them" wanting more. The slot for it was around fifteen minutes, and most congregants would have been happy with 10 minutes, or less, much less even. Mine got considerably more, more than many wanted.

****

There was an old country tale shared with me a few months after my arrival, it was perhaps a hint, I am still not sure, which made this clear.

The story told how on a very cold winter's day, when the snow was piled high and even the farmers struggled to get out and about in their battered old Land Rovers, the minister made his way the short distance to his church next door and opened up for the Sunday service. He wondered how many of the congregation would be able to get there. He soon found out. As the clock struck 11.00am the time the service would normally start there was no one in the church except himself. Just as he was about to give up, walk to the door, lock up and go home, the door opened and in came one of his flock, a farmer who had just been able to make his way down the lane to get to the church for the service. The minister welcomed him and began. He went about his business as if the church was full, all for the benefit of this solitary figure, the farmer who had made it in through the deep snow.

The minister thought to himself, "If he has made the effort to get here in these conditions then the least I can do is to give him a good service." And so it went on: all four hymns, two readings, several prayers and a time for silent contemplation, the notices, even the collection and a long, long sermon, all as usual.

At the end of the service the minister went to the back of the church to shake hands with his congregation of one as he was leaving and the farmer paused.

"Thank you, your Reverence, I really appreciated it. You went to a lot of trouble there. Just for me."

"Not at all," said the minister, "it was my pleasure." "After all, if you went out in the snow to feed your sheep and you could only find one of them, you would not turn it away would you? You would feed it, wouldn't you?"

After a long pause, the farmer looked at the minister, scratched his chin and nodded in agreement. "Aye, this is true your Reverence, this is very true. I would that."

Then after another even longer pause he added, "The difference is I would not give it the whole bloody bucketful."

Seventeen "bad" eggs and offensive embryos, and "a bit too religious for them"

I am afraid I have to confess publicly that I did give my first congregation the "whole bloody bucketful," so to speak. They were lucky to get away with a twenty or twenty-five minute sermon; poor things! To their eternal credit they did not complain. Some of them were to complain about things when it all turned a bit unpleasant towards the end of my ministry. For example, some complained about a visiting preacher I had arranged to cover for me in my absence because of his dreadful, offensive and embarrassing language. Apparently, I was later told, he had referred seventeen times to human eggs and embryos in his sermon on aspects of medical ethics. This lady knew it was seventeen times as she had sat there and counted, she told me. He had upset the congregation was how it was reported to me by another on my return from holiday; this literally a few minutes after we arrived back following a long and tiring journey returning from a few days in England seeing family and friends. I failed to see how the man in question would ever say anything offensive. He was a lovely man, a really gentle man and a gentleman, a Lay Preacher who had served the church many times before when there was a shortage of ministers, or when the minister was away, like I had been for a rare holiday.

Holidays were rare, because we could not easily and with a clear conscience take our allotted time away. I was often told that my predecessors rarely took any time off, perhaps just a week each year to go over to Scotland for a few days. Another thing was that to take a real holiday we had to get away from the manse and we could not afford to do this often. As I explained earlier, to take a holiday from ministry and to stay in the manse, well these two were pretty much mutually exclusive possibilities. If you were there in the manse, you were seen to be in harness, and it was thought by well intentioned congregants and visitors that this one request to talk about a wedding or for a hospital visit was only one request, and what was this one tiny thing out of a whole week? This of course was worked out in ignorance of the other twenty or thirty people who also had just one request. And, should a death occur and you were anywhere in the Province, then it was yours and no mistake about it. The people, your people, your flock, wanted you, and no one else would do.

I once got a telephone call from a senior member of the congregation during the early stages of a family holiday, a visit back to England, to inform me that a lady had died, "Not that I am asking you to come back on Wednesday for the funeral, but I thought that you would want to know." It caused a lot of soul searching: to return or not. I was always left with an awful feeling of guilt, whichever I chose. After this, I made sure never to give out details of our movements, or any of the contact numbers where I might be reached.

****

It was whilst we were on a trip to England that this guest preacher was said to have offended the congregation. But, surely it was not possible that this lovely man had used offensive language in church, as it was reported to me minutes after we had pulled up on the sloping drive down the side of the manse after the long and tiring journey home from England. This man was both a gentleman and a scholar. He lectured at the university. He also had served the denomination and my congregation well for years and he was a popular preacher.

But the complaint had been made and in quite an aggressive and accusing manner, most of which was directed at me rather than the absent preacher who had written and uttered the heinous and offensive words, as I recall. I had the feeling that I was in the frame, that I was being blamed, perhaps, because I had been responsible for arranging for him to come to Moneymore whilst we were away; or was it an indication of something else going on, something which had been brewing in my absence?

After all, the lady who brought the untimely message was quite a sad soul, really. She was "quite simple," it was said to me. I was also told that she "could not be trusted around money," but I felt quite sorry for her as it was obvious to me on a number of occasions that she was used by some to do the donkey work in the church. For example she was made very good use of during the preparations for harvest, or at the regular and arduous cleaning operations which maintained the church to a very high standard. This work was usually overseen and orchestrated by the very same individuals who would then speak badly about her behind her back. They also kept a close eye on her whenever church sales were on or handbags left unattended. I felt she was quite harmless really, but she could be a little brusque rather than aggressive in her manner, and she had been in trouble with the police. She would be again soon after, following a long standing dispute with her neighbour, when I had to get involved with the police on her behalf at 3.00am one morning. I also wondered if she had merely been the message bearer the day she delivered her message to me as I was unloading the car moments after we returned from our holiday.

It wasn't terribly clear to me exactly what had gone on, but I did hear enough to get the picture about how wrong and offensive it was, it was "bad," she said, "bad, all that talk about eggs and the like, in church of all places."

****

This complaint made the moment I arrived back in the village was really quite bizarre, but I had to follow it up. I contacted the man in question and gently probed him about his visit and the sermon in question. It was true it had been about medical ethics, and he had discussed a topic which was then in the public eye. I cannot recall now exactly what it was, but I suspect it was to do with genetic engineering, cloning or abortion, or the like. I did not go into any detail about the so called offence caused. I wanted to spare his feelings. He took my interest to be a genuine academic interest about the issues and offered to send me a copy of his sermon.

Suffice it to say that there was nothing offensive in the sermon. The lady who had been diligent in her counting in church during the sermon was correct: there were seventeen references to eggs or embryos, but nothing in the least bit offensive in it for an adult congregation. More than this, I remember it striking me, and making me laugh, this was a farming congregation. It was made up mostly of people who were dealing with eggs and birth (and death) every day, and in many cases sexing chickens, dealing with cattle teats, perhaps castrating bullocks, even administering artificial insemination, or at least talking of it and more over the dinner table. How could this learned sermon from a gentleman and a scholar have caused any offence by talking about eggs and the like?

****

Thinking of eggs, I do recall with a smile how at one early church social gathering the talk had turned to chickens because Angela had wanted to get some, for, dare I say it again without offending the reader, the eggs they would provide for us. We were in good and expert company, or so we thought. Good country folk who had spent their lives in and around animals and birds. The discussion ranged from the best way of keeping chickens and slaughtering them for table, the best food for them and who currently had some we could have. We were later to pick up six whites, all thrown into a black bin liner for transport home in the back of our car!

The conversation in the church hall continued and we explained that we were not interested in having a cockerel as well because of the noise it would make. We had heard enough crowing at 4.00am. Then a lady in her thirties warned us, quite seriously, that if we got six hens and each laid, say, one egg every day, we could soon be inundated with chicks. We made a discreet exit from the conversation to talk to someone else, just as this lady went bright red as her friend kindly explained to her in lay(wo)man's terms the process involved in fertilizing an egg, and that the eggs would only hatch into chicks if the hen had been near to a cockerel, very near one, actually.

****

Looking back, I think this lack of understanding amongst the farming community was exceptional. I also thought that the so called offence caused by the visiting preacher went much deeper and involved me. The strains of, "Will ye nay come back again" had faded for some, and over the next year, or so, things turned rather unpleasant, degenerating at times into silliness. Some of the congregation, a tiny minority really, were to complain about me wearing shorts when I cut the grass at the front of the manse on a very hot day. I knew my legs were not terrific, but I was shocked to think they were that bad. And a few complained that they "did not want none of that Philosophy stuff here." I had just completed a post-graduate degree in Philosophy and some in ignorance tried to use this to make a negative point.

Until then and very much to their eternal credit, they, for the most part an uneducated farming congregation, suffered my terribly long sermons without a murmur. They suffered in silence. I suspect they thought that such suffering must be doing them some good on some level, perhaps good for the soul? I cannot imagine what I was thinking of?

****

Looking back now, in the knowledge that for some the church is merely a social club or worse a power base, it is perhaps no great surprise that on the day of my Ordination one very senior church member was heard to say about me, "I think he is too religious for us." When I was first told this, long, long after the event, I found it disappointing, a bit hurtful and a huge irony. How can a minister be "too religious," even if his sermons were sometimes overly enthusiastic? And this said on the day of Ordination of all days; a very special day for all concerned; a day when the new minister was not only installed and publicly recognized as the minister, but also Ordained- a grand spiritual occasion. Ordination goes back to the early Church. It is meant to mark someone out, effectively to set them apart with a ritual which is as old as Christianity itself. It involved on this occasion about a dozen brother ministers surrounding me as I knelt at the front of the church facing my congregation-to-be and my colleagues placing their hands upon my head at the same time, invoking God's blessing on me and my ministry.

Afterwards, when asked by a friend of ours from England who visited for the occasion, one of the few who were brave enough to do so, "What did you feel?" I had to be honest. There was no great spiritual outpouring, no dove or voice of approval from on high, just the crushing weight of too many hands resting heavily upon my head. Nevertheless, it publicly marked the start of my ministry, and the time when I was being installed as minister of the church. It was a highly spiritual moment for me and for my congregation, my Calling was affirmed and my appointment as their minister was confirmed. That was when it was said by a key member of my new congregation, "I think he is too religious for us."

A very noisy son welcomed, accompanied by a very noisy band

Special services meant that guests could be invited from other congregations and the church would be packed. The special service was also an opportunity for something different, elaborate even. A special soloist to accompany the church choir perhaps, which, even if we were being charitable, sounded pretty rough and had a wonderful knack for making all tunes and hymns sound the same, or the local brass or silver band to lead and accompany the hymn singing.

It was at a special service of harvest thanksgiving that we had a visiting thirty-piece brass band filling the front of the church, to lead the singing of the harvest hymns and play two or three musical offerings. The band was brilliant, fresh from some major victory in a national (it might even have been international) competition in the big brass band world. The church was packed to overflowing and it was very, very hot. The evening stands out for three reasons.

Firstly, the band was terrific, but my advice is never book a thirty-piece brass band to perform in a packed church. The noise was absolutely deafening, brilliant but quite deafening; and I was sitting directly above and over them in the raised pulpit from where I conducted the service (not the band). The band was far more suited for large outside spaces like a football field, not in a moderately sized place of worship.

The second reason it stands out was that it was the night we decided I should baptise our son, Andy, he of Tipp-Ex fame, and he decided to bawl noisily and incessantly the whole way through the baptism, giving the band a pretty good run for its money.

Thirdly, the evening stands out because one member of the congregation was so overcome by the heat and noise, and perhaps the emotion of the occasion, that she had a very nasty accident of a highly personal nature, right there at the back of the church. It might have been any one of the noise, the heat or the emotions, or all three.

The evening had started so well, with a large congregation gathering a long way ahead of kick off time. I was in the church about an hour before, making sure all was well with the heating and the organist, putting my notes and books on the pulpit stand and so on. I was there to meet and greet the band members who wanted a quick run through of the tunes for the evening. They assembled in one of the church halls a good distance from the church and when I realized that I could hear them through the thick walls and closed doors of both the hall they were in and the church, all at a considerable distance, I began to wonder. Still, mine was not to reason why about such matters. This had been arranged long since by a key member of the congregation who was related to one of the band members, and, as I was told on a number of occasions, it was an honour for us to be hosting them, especially for the harvest service.

****

And so it was, on that night a huge gathering of people, hundreds, filled the beautifully decorated church for the harvest service and to hear the band. The church was full to overflowing, with the band dominating the large empty space at the front, sitting on chairs squeezed around the Communion Table. Every pew bench was crammed with people, and the volunteers who had turned up the previous day to spend much of Saturday dressing the church with the harvest produce had done us proud. Somehow everything was squeezed in, the band, the people, all the produce, including huge amounts of fruit and vegetable, the many displays of flowers and the other harvest decorations.

No one aside from Angela, the girls and I knew that we had an extra surprise in store. We thought that this would be an ideal time to mark Andy's arrival by having his baptism this night. We were well aware that we would not get family members to come over from England for it, and knew we could always do a perfunctory blessing service of some sort back home in England in the near future so that no one would feel left out of the proceedings.

Some people might not have even thought of a having a baptism without all the family being there. Angela and I

244

were not like that. For a start our situation was different. We were far from home and family. More than this we did not hold to any very traditional, high theological, view of the ceremony, such as it involving the washing away of sins, or any insincere promises to reject the devil. This was far too heavy and was never a feature of my beliefs, nor my services of baptism. "How could an innocent baby be born in sin?" I used to ask my congregation on the days I carried out a baptism in my church. It made no sense to me. "Better to marvel at the wonder of life and give thanks for it and wonder at the enormous potential here in my arms," I would say as I walked around the church carrying the baby showing it off to the congregation. In my liberal understanding this ceremony was a public way to recognize the miracle of life and to acknowledge the arrival of a new child, to name it and to welcome it into the church membership in the hope that she or he would wish to be involved in the future.

The other complicated decision we had to make was who should perform the short ceremony, which usually took place during an ordinary service. The problem was this would mean taking a colleague away from his church for the morning or evening, and, more of a problem, who to ask? We could see a disaster waiting to happen. There were a number of colleagues to whom we were very close and would have wanted to perform the ceremony; there were others who we did not particularly desire should do it, but were sort of in the frame because of the pecking order and so on. There was also a degree of rivalry between some of the ministers and so on, and for some ill feeling from long past clashes at meetings and fall outs and the like. It was not always a happy band of pilgrims. After all, ministers are nothing other than human beings, even if they do have that small piece of white plastic as a sign that they are set apart.

There was only one practical solution. I would do it myself. I would baptise my son in my own church in front of my fairly new congregation. What could go wrong?

****

So we thought we would have Andy baptised on the night of the harvest thanksgiving service and that I would do it. It seemed so appropriate, where better to celebrate the birth of our son than amidst our new congregation? We knew that they greatly envied a neighbouring congregation who the previous year had the pleasure and good fortune of sharing such an event with their minister and the new addition to his family. How proud they were and delighted to put on a special tea following the service.

My congregation would be thrilled, I thought, to be surprised like this at the service of harvest thanksgiving. They had dropped enough hints since Andy was born. They hoped the baptism would take place in their midst, rather than across the Irish Sea. After all, he was their Wee-man as they affectionately referred to him. I was wrong.

****

The church was full to overflowing. I was delighted as I made my way in to the sound of the organ. I had begun the short journey to the church that evening, as ever prior to a service, in the Committee Room, a separate building adjacent to the church. This was customary as just before the service was due to begin, perhaps ten or fifteen minutes before, the most senior members of the congregation assembled with me in this Committee Room. I robed up in my Geneva gown, all black of course, and donned my academic hood. At least this injected a little colour as light relief. It was all very formal and sombre. I then offered a short prayer. The walls of this one-roomed, purpose-built building were lined with photographs and paintings of the ministers from the past. The "rogue's gallery," as some of my colleagues referred to it, which existed in most of the churches I visited in the Province. It was a very formal and sombre setting, with the ministers of the past, often with faces and expressions to match the solemn surroundings.

The dozen or so church officers left to take up their places in the church. I was escorted by the most senior member of all, and led, as usual, into the church: always through the same door. The church in fact had three doors. It was formed in the shape of what was called a "broken cross." Door one, the one I entered by for services, faced the pulpit, it was a long walk up the carpeted aisle. At the top end of the church, a large, open space, effectively in front of the pulpit, complete with its seat and a half-door. The pulpit sat up on a high platform, watching over the large open space beneath it. The space was usually empty apart from the Communion Table, but this evening it was

247

completely filled to overflowing with the members of the 30-piece brass band. From the space in front of the pulpit, you could turn right or left and travel a long walk, the same distance either way, to the exit door on the left or the exit door on the right.

I always finished a service by leaving the pulpit during the final hymn, coming forward to the Communion table for the Benediction, the final blessing, and turned to my left and slowly made my way to the door on that side of the church.

Outside, I would make my way to the big, imposing black iron-gates in the church railings, and wait there for my flock to leave the church and queue to file past me, as was the tradition. I would stand there for as long as it took, until I had spoken to and shaken the hand of every single member who left from this door. Some of course slipped out by the other two doors and discretely made their way home for lunch, for often, given my lengthy sermons, it was now way past noon. Many times it was bitter cold, with a bleak, cutting, icy wind blowing up the fields at the back of the church, past the gravestones in the church graveyard, which backed on to one side of the manse (this did spook the kids rather, as they could look straight down into it at night from one of the bedroom windows) and up past the Committee Room, which sort of provided a nice tunnel effect for it to assault me and the people queuing. Even if it was raining, I stood there. I can only recall one occasion when the weather was so awful, with the wind ripping tiles from the roofs, that my church officers and I reluctantly decided that discretion was the better part of valour and today we would let them off.

While the conversations at the gate were fairly trivial and rather public, it did give an opportunity for me to speak to most of my congregation and for them to whisper that they would like to speak to me about something or to inform me that Mrs Y was about to go into, or come out of, hospital, and so on. Occasionally, an elderly or eccentric member would want to chat at length, much to the concern and irritation of the increasingly impatient queue, which had one eye on their watches and the other on their lunch, which was soon to be prepared, or was waiting for them at home, or, much worse still, beginning to burn.

Following these many special services the pattern was a little different. The congregation and visitors would file out of church and walk a few hundred yards across the church grounds and car park to the huge church hall to have their "teas." During the refreshments I would take the opportunity to speak to everyone in the hall and would endeavour to shake as many hands as I could at the end of the evening as people left for home.

This was to be the pattern at the end of the special service of harvest thanksgiving at which I baptised our son. It did not turn out quite like that for one lady of the congregation, for whom the service came to an abrupt and unfortunate end. It would also leave a lasting impression on the most particular and well dressed member of the congregation and his car.

249

The service came to a messy end

On the night of our son's baptism, I was as usual escorted to the church and entered. I can easily recall how spectacular it looked. They certainly knew how to put on a show. It was very impressive. The team of volunteer cleaners had made it sparkle like a new pin, the harvest goods were resplendent, and the band added a touch of colour, even majesty, as they sat their in their navy uniforms and caps, holding their gleaming instruments.

The organist on my nodded command stopped playing the lighter and easy to listen to background music and now the organ thundered out its formal announcement that "His Reverence" had arrived and everyone must stand up, all 400-500 of them.

I made my way with quiet dignity up the aisle towards the pulpit and then slowed up. My usual path to the pulpit was blocked. The final bit of my journey which would take me past the side of the Communion Table and up on to the raised platform, and then nearer to God, we hoped, up the three steps into the pulpit. This was now blocked by the 30-piece brass band.

No one had considered, neither had I, that the seating arrangements for the band were such that when seated, having moved each chair a little to the left or right, or backwards a little, to accommodate a music stand for each member, they would take up all of the available space. Now there was no clear route through for me to get to the pulpit. Not a good start to the evening.

I stood by the first musician I came to and there followed an undignified melee, as I pushed and shoved my way through the band. Most of them tried to get up and ease out of my way, but they were all packed in like sardines. To make it worse my flapping gown got caught on a music stand and pulled it over; it landed on the musician behind, who was taken by surprise, and it fell into pieces, with the music sheets scattering. It was not a good start.

After I finally managed to find my way to the pulpit and gave the band a few minutes to reassemble and to sort themselves out, I was able to announce the first of the harvest hymns, most probably, "We plough the fields and scatter," a much loved favourite on these occasions. The service carried on in a typical fashion, except that the band played a number of musical offerings. They were brilliant, but the noise was deafening. Even next day my ears were ringing. It suited some though, and here I am thinking of the elderly who were a little, or more than a little, hard of hearing, for example, one very deaf lady, who usually sat right at the very back of the church, as far away from me, the speaker, as possible, and then regularly complained to the committee that she could not hear a thing on Sundays. This in spite of a new PA system having been installed quite recently as well as a loop system which was purchased especially to assist those with a hearing aid. This lady, who incidentally had a hearing aid, but never switched it on, came up to me right after the service and thanked me and

251

said it had been wonderful tonight because she had heard the band, nothing else, of course, just the band.

If I thought the noise of the band was to be the only issue to contend with this night, I was wrong.

****

The rest of the service proceeded as normal without much ado, apart from the three or four offerings from the band to get through, and we approached what would have been the end of the service. However, it was getting terribly hot in there. The ancient church heating system, put on a little too late really, there was always an economy drive on, had now, towards the end of the service, started to do its job. The old boiler had cranked up, and now after a couple of hours it was pumping out a tropical heat. This was added to by the sheer number of bodies: the congregation, the band and a lot of visitors who liked to do the rounds, to visit other churches and listen to other ministers at harvest time. Many of the congregation were looking red-faced and flushed. Some were flapping and fanning away at their faces with the extra hymn sheets put out to supplement the hymns book supply which had been exhausted by the huge numbers turning up. Many were discretely trying to slip out of their heavy winter coats and finding it impossible to do so for the lack of space, reluctantly resigning themselves to a very hot last few minutes of the service. At least, soon, they would be out in the cool of the late October air and on the way to the hall, just along the road, for their "teas."

It was at this point I had decided to baptise Andy. Angela, whose absence had been noted by many I am sure, had been waiting in the manse and at the appointed time made her way to the Committee Room and then into the church. The timing was impeccable: bang on cue.

There was a surprised look on many faces, shock on a few, as I announced that tonight I was going to baptise our son. I made my way down to the steps to the front and somehow the band made a clearing for me. They were able to pass instruments to the back and music stands were collapsed as they had now finished their evening's work. A space was made and Angela brought Andy up and stood in front of me.

****

I was very proud as I took my son in one arm and started to read the words of my baptismal service from the folder on the Communion Table. I knew the words very well, of course, and often adlibbed as I went along, as I felt there was nothing worse than someone reading strictly from a script. I knew I would not be able to take my customary walk around the church with my son in my arms, showing him off to the congregation, as there was no space for this. I was content enough to have the small clearing at the front, and I was a very proud dad, indeed, as I started to speak about baptism. And then he started. Andy started.

At this very moment, bored or uncomfortable in the extreme heat, and still pretty much surrounded by all the band members, with all eyes in the church on him, he started to cry. Well, it was more of a scream, really. You know the typical baby scream, when things are not going according to baby's plans, and there is only one way to protest, and that is to open your lungs and scream an angry and very red-faced scream. And the longer it went on the louder it got. It was impressive stuff. He went on and on, and he would not stop.

Now, and here I look back and I feel rather embarrassed, if I had that night used half the brains I was born with I would have handed Andy over to his mum, cut the service short and retired gracefully to the hall for my "teas," as they called it. Alas I did not and it made for a very noisy and messy end to the service in more ways than one.

****

I have already confessed that I was a tad more than enthusiastic in my work, and I was, perhaps, it now dawns on me, more than a little tenacious, stubborn even some might say; but I have always tried in life to plough on towards achieving my goals regardless of obstacles, just like that night when I was driving around Belfast on my quest

254

for a curry for my pregnant wife. I ploughed on regardless. And plough on I did this night, too, the night of my son's baptism. I so wanted to give my son a wonderful baptism, not that he would remember it, of course, but we had arranged for a friend in the congregation to make a tape recording of it, something to present to him in years to come.

It had already been a much longer service than the usual hour and a bit. What with the commotion of me trying to get to the pulpit at the start of the service and the extra offerings belted out by the brass band, we were about 75 minutes in when I announced that I was to baptise my own son. And it was getting hotter all the time.

As I made my way through my material: some opening words about the meaning of baptism, a reading from the New Testament, with Jesus blessing the children, a prayer and the baptismal formula and more prayers, Andy screamed louder and louder, wriggling away in my arms in an attempt to escape; and, I am more than a little embarrassed to tell you, I simply and stubbornly ploughed on regardless. Enthusiastically, naively and probably unfairly to all concerned, I ploughed on to give them, him, the whole "bloody bucketful!"

****

To this day, I am still not sure if anyone heard the content of what I said, but say it I did, until it was all over and done with. I was just dismissing the people with a final blessing, when just at that very moment there was a commotion at the back of the church to my right: a murmur, a thud and a gasp from several people, all followed by some movement, some activity, some whispers.

One more senior lady of the congregation (a spinster lady who looked much older than she really was), a lady who was known to be more than a little eccentric to say the least, had been overcome by the heat and fainted. She had been standing for my final words and then keeled over, falling on top of the lady to her side, and then slipping down to the floor. Not only did she faint, but she had a terrible accident. It was not the sort of accident in which she hurt herself, thank goodness, but the sort which some might say is worse than receiving a physical injury: a personal accident, of the sort where only one's dignity is assaulted.

It might have been the emotion of the service, the heat in the church or being trapped in the pew in the huge crowd, wrapped in a thick winter coat and hat, and perhaps elements of all three played a part in what happened, but I was to find out something more. The next day when I visited her to see if she had made a good recovery from her ordeal she confessed to me that she had taken a triple dose of laxatives just before she left home that evening to come out to church – this about an hour before the service started. I think this was the real reason for the events which brought the service to a rather messy end.

Miss Yates was terribly embarrassed by her ordeal. She was lifted up, guided from the church and helped into the Committee Room, where she was sat down on a chair, leaving a terrible smell in her wake. She recovered quite quickly out of the heat of the church and, perhaps because of her embarrassment at the events, wanted to get home as quickly as possible. But there was no way we could allow her to walk home. I was required to say Grace at the tea in the hall and publicly thank the brass band which was joining us there, and I was already quite late, so I could not take her the short distance to home by car. Just then, by sheer coincidence, the most fastidious member of the congregation, Brian, the man who donated to me his slightly worn Dior and St Laurent suits, put his head in through the door of the Committee Room, and said, "I will take Miss Yates home, I am driving past her house and my car is close by. My wife is in it now and she will help."

Perhaps I should have said something, but it was a genuinely kind gesture, from a kind and generous man. He must have known what he was letting himself in for. However, later, when I thought about it, and after a chat to his wife on the telephone, I was left with a clear picture of him spending days scrubbing out the soft, beige, calf leather, back seat of his car, time and time again. This episode was never mentioned by anyone ever again. Save, next day when Miss Yates confessed to me that she had taken, "three lots of them tablets," adding "perhaps it was them which made me ill last night, Reverend Rowley,

257

perhaps it was them. I knew I should not be taking three lots of them."

It wasn't a glorious end to an action packed service. At the very end of a long evening, when the "teas" were well and truly done and the visitors and congregation had left, I stood chatting to one or two of the church officers. It was obvious that they were not happy about something. Was it poor Miss Yates and her ordeal? Was it the difficulties with the band, perhaps, or their volume? It was neither.

They were unhappy that I had gone ahead and baptised my son without letting them know in advance. Sometimes, it felt, as my surprise backfired, you could not win for trying.

The day two donkeys and a pony came to church

The success of bringing a newborn lamb into church had got me thinking. Remembering how much the children had enjoyed the experience I had a bright idea. I would try to arrange for one of the farmers to bring in a donkey for Palm Sunday. What a great idea I thought. The kids would never forget this, the day a donkey came to church. My committee were not so sure. "Do you know what you are doing?" said one quietly, the first time we were alone after I had proposed it at a meeting. "As long as you are sure, that's all, as long as you are sure?"

I sent out the message that I was looking for a donkey to come to church on Palm Sunday, in two week's time, and the quizzical responses came back, "You mean outside in the car park, of course?" There were some raised eyebrows when I explained that I wanted the donkey to come in to the church and walk the full length of the carpeted aisle, from the door at the end of the aisle on the left of the pulpit, walk right across the front of the church, past the Communion Table in the centre space below the pulpit, the space where the brass band had been so tightly packed in on the night of the harvest thanksgiving service, and, after a pause for some fitting words of wisdom from me, leave down the carpeted aisle on my right and out at the door at the far end; simple.

One local farmer who was not a member of the congregation rang me and said he had heard I was looking for a donkey. He thought I wanted to buy one, he shouted down the phone. He told me he had one for sale, a good beast with plenty of life left in him yet and that he would give me a good price, with me being a man of the cloth. He added that he did not get to his own church as much as he should.

Then a member of the congregation came to see me and said she knew where we could get one, but was I aware that donkeys were quite difficult creatures and more often than not lived up to their name of being stubborn. Great I replied, it sounded just right and could we arrange a practice run on the Wednesday before the Sunday service. The day came and so did the donkey, well almost. It refused to get out of the trailer which had brought it from the nearby farm. No matter how its owner or his daughter, who had come along to help, pulled or coerced it or tried to bribe it with carrots, it would not budge. This was not going according to plan, I thought. The farmer thought for a moment and scratched his head. "He would come on out if Millie was here," he said, thoughtfully. I asked him who Millie was. "It's his friend, the Shetland. Can't separate them ever, ye see. Friends for years. He is missing his friend. That's what it is. That's why he don't want to know. That's why he won't come out. Hang on here and I will go back and

260

get the cattle truck, they will both fit in there with no trouble at all."

So I waited, wondering what I had started. About thirty minutes later the farmer, true to his word, pulled up outside the church with his large cattle truck which easily accommodated the donkey and its best friend Millie, and to my surprise another donkey. Apparently all three lived together in the field and when both the donkey and Mille had been loaded up into the truck the third friend, and I cannot today recall the names of either donkey, only Millie's name, the second donkey created such a fuss that the farmer had no option but to let it climb up into the truck and join the party.

"Now we shall see if I am right," said the farmer. And he was. With Millie in the lead, the stubborn donkey number one was now meek and mild and trotted along like a lamb (please excuse the pun) behind his friend, closely followed by donkey number two. All I wanted was a donkey, one donkey, I thought, now I have got two and a Shetland pony, as well.

****

We processed into the church without any bother at all, except when the organist started up the organ. The organist just happened to be in the church running through the hymns for the special service to come and her eyes were popping out as if on stalks as she saw the church door open and a Shetland come in closely followed by the two donkeys. I am sure it was not in any way a reflection on her playing or her choice of hymn or tune, but just as the second donkey reached level with the pulpit, just in front of the Communion Table, it paused, swished its tail up and evacuated its bowels right there on the church carpet. The farmer who was leading the troupe looked terribly embarrassed and started to pull the Shetland more quickly to hasten their departure from the church. The organist, who was a rather prim and proper lady, looked rather shocked.

I went outside and thanked the farmer for his time and trouble as he was loading the animals into the truck, with the help of his daughter. "I am so sorry, your Reverence, so sorry about that. All that muck in there. In the church an all. What will the committee say?" He added, "I suppose this means you won't want us to come along on Sunday now?" After a brief pause and a silent prayer, I made a bold decision. The church was as much for the children as it was for anyone else. "Of course I want you to come on Sunday. After all the trouble you have been to today. And I wouldn't want to hurt their feelings," I said nodding in the direction of the three heads which were staring straight at us from the back of the truck, "I think they enjoyed it."

I waved them off and went into the manse, boiled some water, put it in a large bucket, added some shampoo and disinfectant, gathered up a hand brush, a broom and a spare bucket and made my way back into the church. I opened the door and made my way to the piles of evidence. The donkey had been pulled along, remember, to the strains of the organ playing the tunes of the Palm Sunday hymns, by the increasingly worried farmer, who for some reason felt responsible. I spent the next hour cleaning the church carpet.

****

Next morning I gingerly went into the church to see if there were any signs of damage after my clean-up operation. Was there any stain, or colour loss to be seen? Had a white patch appeared in the middle of a dark red carpet, or was there any shrinkage? But, much to my relief, all was well, and even a well trained eye would not have been able to detect any sign of the donkey's distress when the organ played up. The carpet had scrubbed up pretty well, even if I say so myself.

I lost more than a little sleep over the next three nights, I can tell you. A couple of times I woke in the early hours of the morning with visions of two donkeys and a pony defecating in the church, once I am sure on the Communion Table itself, all whilst being chased around the church by the unsmiling and angry committee members. At times, even in waking moments, I was sure it would go horribly wrong and I would be to blame. You see the church was almost, if not quite, holy ground for many; not so much I felt then for overtly religious reasons, although this would have played a part for some, but for lots of people it was a special place because it had been the place where generations of family members had been baptised, married or buried. It was a place of special memories. The congregation loved the place and tended it with great enthusiasm. This was especially true of the committee members who were the appointed guardians of the church and its finances. To their credit they took their duties very seriously, giving up an awful lot of their time to ensure the true and upright running and upkeep of the church, the hall, the old school, which had been the village school run by the church, and the impressive array of outbuildings. They were especially effective at managing the church finances and every penny spent was debated and, at times, disagreed over. Of the many of the farming community I met, some could be extremely generous with their time and efforts, and with their money for a good cause. Others were not so easily parted from their money.

****

I am more than happy to record, much to my relief then and now, that the visit of the stubborn donkey number one, his friend Millie the Shetland and donkey number two, who was not going to miss out, went like a dream. After talking to the children about Palm Sunday in front of a very large congregation, and on my nod, with very few of the congregation knowing what to expect, the party of three visitors, meekly trotted in the one door, led by the farmer's daughter, with the farmer at the rear, carrying a bucket and small spade, would you believe. They made their way along the aisle, past the pulpit and Communion Table, and straight down the opposite aisle and then out of the church. Common sense had made me abandon the original arrangement and so they did not stop in the front of the pulpit or pause at any time. It was not worth the risk, not with a full church, plus the presence of the full Church Committee, who protected the property for all they were worth. It worked a treat. The three visitors behaved impeccably and there were no accidents for which to be held accountable.

I breathed a huge sigh of relief when this service was over with no damage done. It was a risk which paid off. Everyone in the congregation, young and old alike loved it. After the service the children rushed outside to feed the visitors carrots. There were two minor problems which arose. Firstly, I was a glutton for punishment and there and then decided to organize an animal blessing service in church, where the congregation would have the chance to bring their pets to a service. Looking back this was more than a little naive given many of my congregation made their living by raising animals for the table. But plan it I did and it did happen in due course.

People think I am joking or exaggerating when I say that I held an animal blessing service in church BEFORE it appeared in one of the early episodes of the Vicar of Dibley. To me, a lover of animals and vegetarian since I was twelve years of age, it seemed a very natural thing to do. I am not claiming it was an original idea, and I probably heard of it somewhere and then developed my own version of it, but the idea was not spawned from watching that episode shown as part of the very first series of the Vicar of Dibley in 1994. By then we had left Moneymore, as that first very warm welcome had turned rather hot, for we had dared to challenge or disagree with some of the most prominent church members once too often for comfort.

The second issue and it is a mere detail, hardly worth mentioning perhaps, but I will as it still makes me smile. As the church door opened on my signal and the special guests entered to many "ooohs" and "aaahs," the organist suddenly, off her own back and quite unplanned, decided to play the tune to Eric Boswell's well known *Little Donkey*. A nice touch to accompany the trio as they made their way into the church, it seemed; but I was more than a little concerned that the organ striking up would have a similar laxative effect on donkey number one, or worse still, I recall thinking, as I stood there suddenly feeling very vulnerable as it crossed my mind it might have the same effect on

Millie the Shetland and donkey number two, as well. Luckily it did not.

What did happen was that some of the children started an impromptu rendition of *Little Donkey*. And then some of the congregation joined in. What was wrong with that, you might ask? Nothing really, but standing there waiting for the accidents which never came, listening to my congregation singing *Little Donkey*, I did wonder about a certain irony as they sang out the words:

"Little donkey, little donkey on the dusty road
Got to keep on plodding onwards with your precious load
Been a long time, little donkey, through the winter's night
Don't give up now, little donkey,
Bethlehem's in sight

Ring out those bells tonight
Bethlehem, Bethlehem
Follow that star tonight
Bethlehem, Bethlehem"

Little Donkey is of course a Christmas carol. As I stood there the irony of it struck me, if not my congregation. They carried on singing the well known Christmas carol:

"Little donkey, little donkey, had a heavy day
Little donkey, carry Mary safely on her way
Little donkey, little donkey, journey's end is near
There are wise men waiting for a sign to bring them here

Do not falter little donkey, there's a star ahead
It will guide you, little donkey, to a cattle shed

Ring out those bells tonight
Bethlehem, Bethlehem"

And so it went on. We got all the verses, more or less perfect, from memory. With the last one timed to perfection as our visiting trio exited by the far door and then the people clapped. The irony was they had just sung a Christmas Carol on Palm Sunday, the day set aside to mark Jesus' humble arrival in Jerusalem on a donkey for Passover, and this on a very mild, very sunny day in mid-April.

As always, it is the thought that counts.

A final tale: the worm turning in the light of the candles

Many more experiences stand out for me as I look back on those years and reflect on the hundreds of services I conducted during my time in Northern Ireland. One lasting memory is the evening I put on something special in the lead up to Christmas: a candlelight carol service, in spite of the concerns expressed about burning down the church. It was also the time when major differences with some of the congregation become apparent.

It was about three years into my ministry and I had been thinking about the Christmas period which was looming and wanted to do something a little different. I had already instigated a Christmas morning service, a shortened version of the usual service, starting earlier than normal at 10.00am, (the normal service started at 11.00am for nine months of the year, but changed to noon for three months in the summer to accommodate the dairy farmers' milking routine). The idea was for a short service, lasting for half an hour or so; a service in which a couple of hymns, prayers and readings were packaged around the children coming up to the front to show me and the congregation their Christmas presents. In addition I gave a short talk (and I do mean short), just a few off-the-cuff words about the real meaning of Christmas.

Even on Christmas Morning, the formality of first meeting in the Committee Room was strictly adhered to and I was led into the church as usual. I was delighted that the service proved to be so popular and we had a congregation of double the normal size. On the back of this success I decided to try something a little bit different; something that the congregation and many visitors would enjoy; something to bring our focus on to the warmth and light of Christmas. After all, the day I put my idea before the church officials in order to check that everyone would agree with it, we all agreed Christmas seemed to be becoming more and more about material things and this would be a wonderful and meaningful way to offset this.

My idea was fairly simple really and hardly inspirational or cutting edge. I suggested we should have an extra service one evening just before Christmas. A service where the church would be bathed in the natural light of hundreds of candles: a simple service of carols by candlelight, followed by mince pies and tea and coffee in the hall. As far as I could see it was a lovely idea, the congregation would rally to it, as always, the church would look wonderful for all the many visitors, as usual, and everyone would share in a wonderful occasion. On top of this I suggested the collection should go to a local charity, a children's home. This was readily agreed by the church hierarchy, and so it all seemed set for another lovely evening, during which we would raise some money for a good cause. What could possible go wrong; there was nothing dangerous or sinister about it, was there? Yet again the Province, or more accurately some of the people in it, would amaze me.

****

270

Aside from the risk of burning down the church, or someone being injured, which was discussed at great length at more than one subsequent committee meeting, little did I know there was some disquiet about it. A disquiet being generated by one of the committee members who had agreed to the idea in the first meeting, but had not voiced his concerns then or at the numerous subsequent planning meetings for the event. It seems there were other more surreptitious ways to make his feelings known.

The fears of burning down the church or anyone being burnt on the night were allayed when it was decided that several of the younger and fit and active male members of the congregation were to be on "firewatch," as some of the older committee members put it, using the term they probably had not uttered since the end of the war, at that time nearly fifty years before.

****

On the afternoon of this special service a large number of volunteers arrived in the church to dress it and the hall for the evening carols by candlelight service and the tea which would follow. This was the time to put up the huge Christmas tree which was always a feature and other Christmas knick-knacks and decorations of an appropriate nature, such as holly wreaths and Christmas floral displays.

271

The hall was made over with all the usual decorations, tinsel and at least two more trees fully dressed and lit.

I was surprised to see on my first Christmas vacation visit a large plastic snowman figure placed at the front of the church. This was plugged into the mains and when switched on it lit up and the snowman's arm moved up and down. I though it was a strange thing to have in a church, but it had been donated by a generous member of the congregation out of kindness and each year was wheeled out to have pride of place.

On the night of the carol service, it was once again placed at the front, waving at all who came in.

Aside from the plastic snowman, the church looked wonderful. All around the window ledges stood candlesticks and holders of all shapes and sizes. We had begged and borrowed these from all over, and I was told by a few people that some had been "stolen" from neighbours for the occasion, both candles and candle holders. We had acquired scores of candle holders and two big cardboard boxes by one of the doors held hundreds of candles which members of the congregation had been donating for two or three weeks, dropping off two or three candles at a time, or larger packs of six or ten. To prevent the glass in the window cracking with the heat, sheets of cooking foil was put up to act as a barrier, and it would also reflect the warm glow of the candles back into the church.

We set to work setting it all out and the final task was for me to climb up the rickety old set of ladders, the same set I had used to paint the manse pink, to dress the two great crystal chandeliers which dominated the space high above the centre of the church over the Communion Table and Pulpit. These must have provided the original lighting inside the church before electricity was around and whilst they served only an ornamental function now, they still had their candle holders intact, only now unused.

These were lovingly filled with the choicest of red candles, twelve in each, all matching as befitted the central display, and we even lined the holders with foil and created a sort of small lip or cup in order to prevent molten wax from dripping onto the church carpet below, near to the several places the donkey had disgraced itself during the private rehearsal for Palm Sunday back in April, some eight months before.

****

We had worked out it would take several people about ten minutes to light all of the candles in time for the service to start. We had candles of every shape and size and quality and could not take the chance that the smaller ones would burn down to their holders and go out, leaving some areas with very low lighting and people unable to see the hymn books, or worse set fire to one of the holders which was not made of metal. We had to get our timing right to allow for the maximum amount of light for the maximum amount

273

time, and we got it about right. Towards the end of the evening some candles did burn down and start to burn the cheaper holders, but the "fireman" on watch in that aisle did his job and soon scooped the whole display safely into his bucket of water.

We kept some of the church lights on as people began to arrive in the church car park for the service. At about twenty-five minutes to the hour the team of "candle-lighters" went to work. Then, finally, with about 15 minutes to go until the start of the service, the church lights were turned off.

****

Quite a sight greeted the congregation and guests as they made their way into the church. The church looked truly magical. The two spectacular crystal chandeliers, which dominated the centre of the church and which were always guaranteed to produce admiring comments at the best of times, now, adorned with twenty-four candles looked truly spectacular, truly magical.

It was a lovely evening. All of the visitors left the hall after having their "teas" with a smile and a word of praise for the evening service. I know because I shook the hand of every single one of them, as was custom. I also spoke to every one of the entire congregation.

274

It was a long night. The majority were delighted with the evening and thanked me for my efforts. But I noticed there was an uneasy disquiet about one or two who seemed to be unusually reluctant to engage me in conversation. And I had noticed one or two talking in whispers in the corners of the room. I was not sure what it was, but I could detect that something was afoot. I was not overly troubled by this. After all it had been a wonderful evening and a resounding success. The church had looked wonderful and been packed to the rafters with visitors. The band, not a big brass band, but a representation of the local flute band, had been superb, playing quietly, or should I say in a fitting manner for the size of the church. And we had raised a lot of money, well over £1000, I recall, for the nominated children's charity.

I was exhausted, as these things could be an emotional drain, not only in the energy spent running around making sure everything went well and worked like clockwork, but also in talking to so many people and the strain of worrying that nothing serious would go wrong. So I left and walked down the road to the manse and bed.

****

It was early next morning that she came to see me. A lady who had welcomed us warmly and supported us fully ever since we first arrived on the summer pastorate. A life

275

long member of the congregation, as her parents had been before her and before them generations of family members. She said she felt she had to come and speak to me and she was quite distressed. Sitting in the front room of the manse, now with a cup of tea in her hands, this lady had come as a friend to tell me what was being said, of the talk which had started last evening immediately after the service, even before it, I was told.

This lady was nearly in tears. She did not want to say the words. I coaxed it out of her. "Come on now, Mrs Durcan, what was being said?"

"Oh Reverend Rowley, it was Mr Gurney, I heard him myself, just after the service, and it was so lovely and all, and so many people. My friend came along and she said it was a lovely service and so much money taken for those poor wee children."

I cut in, "What is it Mrs Durcan, what is upsetting you so much. What did he say?"

She paused, gulped and had tears in her eyes as she turned to me and said, "Reverend Rowley, he was going around telling people that the candles, all those lovely candles in church, that it was wrong." Another pause, as if she could hardly bring herself to utter the words. He said, "It was a shameful act of popery."

****

276

"A shameful act of popery," he called it. 'Popery' was an offensive term, a noun describing the doctrines, practices, and rituals of the Roman Catholic Church. There had once even been a Popery Act, passed in Ireland in 1703 (repealed six years later), in order to influence an inheritance being passed on in a Roman Catholic family. For these years the estate had to be divided equally between all of the sons, and there could be many, unless the eldest converted from his faith to the Protestant faith, when he could claim it all.

And here was I effectively being called a papist (yet another disparaging term used for a Roman Catholic); all because we had used candles in the church.

What might seem laughable to me now, and to anyone who reads this, it was quite chilling at the time. This was not only very far from the truth, for whilst I, as a liberal, saw value of some kind in most religious teachings, Christian and otherwise, as long as they brought out the best in the adherents, I was most certainly not some secret sympathizer and supporter of the Roman Catholic Church, its teaching, practices and rituals, nor of its leader, the Pope.

Not only was it far from the truth, it was dangerous. Given the situation at the time when people were being killed for happening to be Roman Catholic or Protestant, killed for being in a pub in a Roman Catholic village or in a Protestant owned fish and chip shop on a Saturday

277

afternoon; talk using the word 'popery' was dangerous talk, indeed.

When Mrs Durcan had composed herself and left, I thought about this for a while and then decided to get on with the day's work, visiting homes and hospitals, and so on, and there was a meeting to attend that night. A busy day ahead, I pondered, better just get on with it. Somehow I knew that I had not heard the last of this claim that my work in suggesting and organizing such a lovely service which raised so much money for such a good cause was nothing other than 'popery.'

****

If I ever reflect on the experience of my ministry in Northern Ireland to determine what went wrong I often look back and highlight this as one of the turning points. After all, you either kicked with the left leg or the right leg and there was nothing in between, as the lady had said.

What a great pity, said Mrs Durcan, the church had looked so "well" and "everyone had enjoyed it so much. What a pity."

And, all for the sake of a few candles.

EVEN HOTTER UNDER THE COLLAR

By Andrew Rowley

It was indeed a very chilling moment when I answered a telephone call in the middle of the night. Standing in the cold kitchen of the manse, I heard the voice of a desperate caller, who would not give her name. She asked me a question. My first thought was, am I being set up to encourage someone, perhaps the caller, to grass on terrorists and then be targeted myself for it? Her question was:

"What shall I do, Reverend Rowley? If I tell the police or the Army and <u>they</u> find out <u>they</u> will kill me and my family. But if I say nothing, many people are going to die. What shall I do? What do you say I should do?"

****

On hearing of the rumours that were beginning to spread around the congregation about the sexual tendency of one of the younger ladies of the congregation, the elderly lady said to me, in a very shocked, indignant and very definite manner, implicitly suggesting perhaps a form of social cleansing:

"We will have none of these lesbeens here, Reverend Rowley, so we won't. We don't want it here and we won't have it."

****

At the start of an official meeting of my church congregation and the church hierarchy from the area, a meeting which I was not allowed to attend, called to try to deal with the growing difficulties and tensions in the congregation about my ministry. Following a pompous and legalistic opening few words from a minister who seemed to revel too much in the power of his role, warning those gathered, in a way more befitting the 17th century, that this was in effect a Church Court and no one could speak without his permission, a farmer's voice from the very back of the hall shouted his derision:

"Catch y'rself on, why don't ye. Catch y'rself on."

****

Even Hotter Under the Collar is the continuing, true saga of a young English minister and his young family as they struggle to cope with life in Northern Ireland and Andrew with his ministry to the country congregation of Moneymore Church, a small Protestant village on the outskirts of Belfast.

In *Even Hotter Under the Collar*, Andrew shares more true stories from his five-year ministry in Northern Ireland during the Troubles. He picks up the story from where he left off in *Hot Under the Collar* and tells us of more of terrorist activity, how things were beginning to go wrong for him with some of his congregation and how it finally led to their departure from the Province and a return to England.

In *Even Hotter Under the Collar,* he also tells us of two major trips he took away from the Province during his ministry there: one to Romania, just after the fall of Ceausescu, in an attempt to try to adopt an orphan following the horrific TV and newspaper reports of the atrocious conditions of many of the orphanages in Romania and the plight of the orphans at the time, and the other, in complete and utter contrast, to America; this for Andrew to conduct an anniversary service at Northwich Presbyterian Church, Arizona. The latter was an all expenses paid, seventeen-day trip, for all of the family, a busman's holiday, offering the hard-up family a wonderful experience, one they could never have afforded on a minister's wage. It was they describe it, "Like winning a top competition prize."

However, on his return he found that all hell had broken out amongst his congregation, and that his ministry there was on borrowed time.

******

If you enjoyed **Hot Under the Collar** and its blend of the sunny and dark side of human nature, and the tales of tragedy and comedy found within the rich tapestry of life, you will enjoy this just as much if not more, for it is getting even hotter for Andrew and his family.

****

Lightning Source UK Ltd.
Milton Keynes UK
UKOW031032100113

204680UK00001B/3/P